S0-BRQ-717

Gift of the
SAMUEL P. HUNT FOUNDATION

Daniele Baroni
Antonio D'Auria

KOLO MOSER
Graphic Artist
and Designer

RIZZOLI
NEW YORK

First published in the United States of America in 1986 by
RIZZOLI INTERNATIONAL PUBLICATIONS, INC.
597 Fifth Avenue, New York, NY 10017

Copyright © 1984 Nuove Edizioni Gabriele Mazzotta
Essays: © 1984 Daniele Baroni and Antonio D'Auria

English language translation Jon Van de Grift and Hanna Hannah

ISBN 0-8478-0667-7
LC 85-43052

Printed and bound in Italy

Contents

Two Reclining Nudes,
1912-15. (Hochschule
für angewandte Kunst,
Vienna)

Reclining Nude, ca.
1912. (Collection J.
Hummel, Vienna)

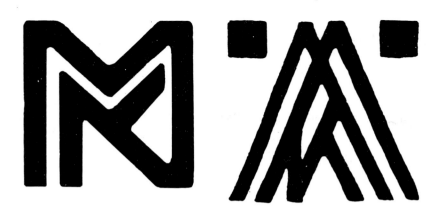

Graphics and Figural Works

Daniele Baroni

A *"Wiener Kind," from the Drawing Table to the Atelier*

"I was born in Vienna in 1868. I grew up near the Theresianum, a famous academy for the sons of Austrian aristocrats and the families of functionaries. My father worked there as financial advisor, a kind of administrator, and I could come and go as I pleased. The Theresianum was a little world in itself. It had spacious parks, pools, and laboratories. Its inhabitants were trained artisans who carried out their work there—or at least during that time they did. Later, many would marvel at my technical versatility in many trades, and at my extensive knowledge of carpentry, bookbinding, and metalworking. I owed it all to my youth and to the appointees of the Theresianum. Everybody knows that a child gets into everything. When he sees something, he learns it immediately. In just this way I learned from the most diverse masters: I bound books, built rabbit hutches, sewed clothes, learned how to cut wood on a lathe and, from the gardener, I learned how to create the most wonderful flower arrangements."[1]

These are Kolo Moser's recollections of his formative years. His father wanted him to go into business, but the boy secretly took lessons in design. In 1885 he took the entrance examination for the Art Academy, and, at 17, began his formal training. Beginning in 1888, as we will see, Moser began his associations with the *Wiener Mode*, and so his first graphics themes appear. He entered the Kunstgewerbeschule in 1892. Soon afterwards he began to serve as tutor to the children of Karl Ludwig of Erzherzog at Wartholz Castle. A connection in Germany was also established when Moser was asked to illustrate books for the publisher Schreiber at Esslingen.

"At that time, Austria had few opportunities to offer my generation. The 'Makart Style' still reigned, with its art of imitation and its ridiculous dusty bouquets. A new wind was blowing in Germany, however, and our generation willingly snatched up those leaflets that Lichwark published in Hamburg."

In 1895 the publisher Martin Gerlach offered some projects to Moser, and through this association the young artist met Gustav Klimt. Moser was among the founding members of the "Club of Seven" (Siebner Club), to which Josef

[1] The autobiographical passages reported here are derived from "Mein Werdegang," published by Kolo Moser in *Velhagen und Klasings Monatshefte*, n. 10, 1916. The title of this chapter refers to the same autobiography entitled *Vom Schreibtisch und aus dem Atelier* in the catalogue from an exhibition called "Kolo Moser—1868-1918." This exhibition was held at the Hochschule für angewandte Kunst in Vienna in 1979. The catalogue was edited by O. Oberhuber and J. Hummel, with a foreword by J. Spalt and W. Mrazek and an essay by W.J. Schweiger.

Maria Olbrich also belonged. Soon the group would be acknowledged by the Künstlerhaus, then the most prestigious association of Austrian artists. "In Vienna, as well, the art world began to stir together with all of the youthful forces that up until that time had been dissatisfied with the conditions around them united in the 'Hagen Group,' named after the owner of the inn where they would meet. Members included Josef Engelhart, Carl Moll, Wilhelm Bernatzik, and all of the future founding members of the Secession. The 'Secession—Vereinigung bildender Künstler Österreichs,' founded in March 1897, signaled the beginning of a new artistic era in Austria. The cause—apart from essential artistic questions—was the unchanging monotony of the Künstlerhaus, which by that time had lost its support. I myself was one of the dissatisfied, along with Helmer, Klimt, Engelhart, Moll, Olbrich, and Hoffmann. The elderly Rudolf von Alt became our first president, and in March of the succeeding year we held our first exhibition in the rooms of the Gartenbau. It was a sensation. This exhibition exposed a large sector of the public to such artists as Meunier, Rodin, Khnopff, Whistler and Puvis de Chavannes."

Figure study, ca. 1890. (Private Collection, Vienna)

"The following year I was able to exhibit at Weinzeile. Olbrich had made a small white temple for us, with the characteristic gold-leaf work. This was the talk of Vienna for some time. There was much joking about the principles of our new use of discrete and quite stylized ornament. We proved to be right in the end, however, and the joking ceased."

Moser executed relief decorations for the Secessionhaus designed by Olbrich. On the rear wall he created a two-dimensional relief of dancing wreath-bearers in white and gold. The side walls ended in two pilasters topped by owls masquerading as capitals—something of a visual joke.

In a long sequence of exhibitions held at the Secession house, Moser planned four solo shows and eight shows with Hoffmann. He participated in two exhibitions. For the fifth and thirteenth he created a poster; for the fifth, thirteenth, and nineteenth, a catalogue. He also revealed his capabilities as an architectural designer.

In 1898 Moser participated in the creation of *Ver Sacrum* and began a profitable relationship with Hoffmann. At this time he also made contact with the Porzellanverlenger Böch, who would be of great importance to him and to his whom he would work at the Kunstgewerbeschule. The following year, in fact, Moser was called to the school by Freiherr von Myrbach as an instructor and, in 1900, as professor.

Moser's young disciples were given the opportunity to take part in the fifteenth Secession exhibition in 1902. The following year the best of the Viennese students exhibited with Moser: Bakalowits for glass, Prag Rudniker for furniture, Backhausen for textiles, and also Carl Geylings Erben, Tiscler Ungethüm, Seidl, Otto Müller, Ludwig, and Schmidt. Public appreciation grew unexpectedly for the new furniture, textiles, and book bindings, and from then on merchants could not meet the great demand for Secessionist work. "It became fashionable, and turned into an industry. Cheap imitations done with little taste appeared, and were so prevalent that the period in Vienna has been dubbed the 'false Secession,' rightly repudiated by Hermann Bahr. The Secession exhibition of 1899 was decisive for the craft movement in Vienna. For the very first time, the latest in Viennese fashion—exemplified by the furniture of Olbrich and Hoffmann, the furniture textiles that I designed for Viennese merchants, works in metal and wood hitherto not preserved—were viewed in the context of current Viennese taste."

Between 1899 and 1900 the publisher Anton Schroll issued the first series of Viennese embroidery designs (*Wienerkunststickereien*) on which Moser worked. Moser also designed a calender for Fromme and made some glass windows for Hoffmann's firm, commissioned for the home of August Lederer. In the eighth Secession exhibition Mackintosh and the Glasgow group, and Ashbee, van de Velde and the Maison Moderne appeared for the first time in Vienna under the title of "European Handicrafts." The Viennese took notice of the "complicated splendor of Wagner, the elegant logic of Hoffmann, and the good poetic taste of Moser."[2] After this initial contact with a more international sphere, Moser, as did others, particularly Charles Rennie Mackintosh and Hoffmann, adopted a more rigorous geometric style. Remarked Hermann Bahr, "For the Viennese, Kolo Moser had been a man of the square; most people believed that he had invented the chessboard."[3] And Bertha Zuckerkandl said that "he became popular in Vienna through his square-shaped patterns; popular, naturally, in the sense of the greatest popular sensation."[4]

Late in 1901, Moser first became involved with the theater through the Jung-Wiener Theater zum lieben Augustin, founded by Felix Salten. In addition to the poster, Moser designed a stage stripped of traditional ornament, using the curtain alone as the sole decorative structure. In 1902 he took part in the XIV Secession Exhibition with two glass windows and a mosaic. After his experience working for the Wiener Kunst im Haus, he and Hoffmann were appointed artistic directors of the Wiener Werkstätte, with Fritz Wärndorfer as administrative and financial director. "We began very modestly, with works in metal; only later would things evolve in ways we couldn't have dreamed. The Wiener Werkstätte was destined to be the center of artistic work guided above all by good sense, good taste, and in particular, by an honest approach. Our first success came not in Vienna, but from the outside, in Berlin where we had prevailed from the start. The placement of our work at the great Hohenzollern store led to our first complete apartment design. Adolphe Stoclet, a Belgian businessman, commissioned Hoffmann to design an urban villa, a country home and a tomb, and the work was assigned to the Wiener Werkstätte. Even greater success awaited us in London and Dresden. The taste for black and white that dominated nearly all of our work seemed rather cold at first, but soon enough the pleasing contrast that it made with the false warmth of the wallpaper was appreciated."

In 1904 Moser became co-editor as well as collaborator of the periodical *Hohe Warte*. Presented here for the first time was the "Arbeitsprogramm" edited

[2] L. Hevesi, *Acht Jahre Sezession*, Vienna, Carl Konegen, 1906.
[3] H. Bahr, *Tagebuch 1918*, Innsbruck/Vienna/Munich, Tyrolia, 1919.
[4] B. Zuckerkandl-Szeps, "Erinnerungen an Kolo Moser," in *Neues Wiener Journal*, 23 January 1927.

by Hoffmann, which related programmatically the activities of the Wiener Werkstätte. Moser also collaborated on the periodical *Der Liebe Augustin*. He was given the task of designing the graphics for the official book celebrating the Jubilee of the Emperor Franz Joseph. Moser designed the filigree work for the card, the cover, and the jacket, as well as the stamp type. Ludwig Hevesi commented on the book in his *Kunst und Kunsthandwerk*: "From the beautiful strands of filigree to the skin of the binding, all stems from the same unitary intellect. A magnificent work that does honor to the firm as well as its collaborators."[5] For Moser, however, the great event of 1904 was his commission to design the altar for the chapel at Steinhof Hospital—even if, as will be seen, Moser's work was later condemned for its lack of religiosity, leading to several surprises and a lawsuit.

Early in 1907, after a few years of frenetic work and intense collaboration with Hoffmann, Moser suddenly abandoned the Werkstätte. "It seemed to me that the work had grown excessive and depended too much on the taste of those who commissioned it. And very often the public had no idea what it wanted. These impossible demands and differences of opinion forced me to quit the Wiener Werkstätte." However, it was not a complete break for Moser: his designs continued to be used, and after his withdrawal from society he returned to his first artistic activity as a painter.

Ornamental motifs with owls and masks designed by Moser for the Olbrich House at the Secession, 1898.

At first it was uncertain whether Moser would collaborate on designs for the Cabaret Fledermaus, despite the fact that he was still Hoffmann's partner. However, at the beginning of the 1907-08 season, he created a costume for Gertrude Barrison, and he also designed costumes for the dancers in *Die Fledermaus*, and for Brattie Young and Nelly Moyse.

In the Kunstschau 1908 uniting the circle of artists around Klimt, Moser was active as an interior designer, in creating the "Klimt Hall, Room 22: Gustav Klimt's Temple to Modern Art." According to Hermann Bahr, there were three great works in the exhibition: "new paintings by Klimt, Moser's drawings for Wagner's Steinhof Church and the Hall of Theatrical Art."[6] After Klimt, Moser was without doubt the best represented artist in the exhibition, and he continued to be well represented in various different projects thereafter: "Among all of the works with which I was commissioned, I must say that the Austrian stamp designs and some set designs gave me the most joy and satisfaction. The Grand Jubilee of 1904 had already given me the chance to work for the Austrian State Typographer. Following this I was invited to design the landscapes for the stamps for Bosnia. Since these were so well received I was then asked to design all of the stamps for Austria. With regard to the theater I had already had some experience a few years earlier with the writer Felix Salten, founder of the ill-fortuned and short-lived 'Jung Wiener Kabarett,' titled 'Zum lieben Augustin.' I had another opportunity in theater design with *Der Musikant* by the Austrian author and composer Julius Bittner at the Hofhoper in Vienna. I also collaborated with Bittner for *Bergsee*, a work by Pfitzner, and at the request of Hermann Bahr I created set designs for his comedy *Das Prinzip*. For

[5] L. Hevesi, in *Kunst und Kunsthandwerk*, n. 8, 1905.
[6] H. Bahr, *Tagebuch*, Berlin, 1909.

Study for a frieze with garland bearers for the posterior facade of the Secession House, 1898. (Private Collection, Vienna)

the most part I painted. Public commissions were quite rare in this area, and the painting for these was impersonal with mass appeal."

Moser held his first solo show at the Miethke Gallery in Vienna in 1912, after those of Klimt and Carl Moll. For all of his multifaceted talent, however, Moser was considered to be more of a craftsman than a painter.

During the following years he continued to work intensively as a set designer for several theatrical projects, winning more criticism than acclaim. Under Bahr's patronage, Moser increasingly turned to literature, especially the legends of Goethe. He was particularly taken with the *Farbenlehre*: "I remember," noted Bahr, "that in a conversation long ago, he was adamant about the *Farbenlehre* because he found premonitions of all the secrets of his art..."[7]

In 1913 Moser met repeatedly with Hodler and held in a series of exhibitions in Budapest, Rome, Düsseldorf and Mannheim. In the following year, he presented an exhibition of set design in Zürich; then he returned once again to applied art. After doing a series of stamps for Bosnia Erzegovina in 1912, he designed stamps for the war. His *curriculum vitae* appeared in 1916, and in the same year he contracted an incurable disease of the larynx, from which he eventually died on 18 October 1920.

The Early Works of Moser: Classicism, Symbolism, Allegory, and Popular Literature

The death of Moser's father in 1888 seems to mark the beginning for Moser of a life of continuous artistic activity. The collaboration that Moser began with the journal *Wiener Mode* and *Meggendorfer Humoristischen Blättern*,[8] for which he designed the costumes, is of great importance. His first graphics stem from an academic tradition of naturalistic form that was typical of the last decades of the century. They are rendered without much interpretation, with a decisive and nervous line. The representation of the figure is always academic but assured and done in a compositional style that reveals his tutelage in a more elegant tradition. This orientation is also confirmed by Moser's student charcoal drawings, especially his representations of the posing figure.

The year 1895 is crucial: it marks in Moser's style and expression a clear break from his scholastic and academic training. During this time he traveled to Munich and immersed himself in the local artistic circles. This Bavarian city was then experimenting with the avant-garde in all the arts, the movement which would be called the Jugendstil. The journal *Jugend*, in fact, began publication at this time. Also part of the avant-garde was the advent of Symbolism, of which Franz von Stuck was the major representative. Von Stuck and Max Klinger forged a new mythology of Mediterranean and Manneristic culture, and were advocates of an eclecticism that repudiated the kitsch of the period.

The publisher Martin Gerlach invited Moser to collaborate on a work called *Allegorien-Neue Folge*. This was a collection of pictures by theme, for which Moser designed eleven on the subjects of love, song, music, dance, all sports

[7] H. Bahr, *Tagebuch 1918*.
[8] For the Schreiberrischen Verlag of Esslingen, Germany.

and fishing in particular. These were composed originally through free association; then they were methodically arranged and paginated. The representations remained naturalistic, but were more ornamental and decorative than in his earlier work. The figure was still the result of an "in the round" approach, with grey tones, graduating shade, and cross-hatching that emphasized the construction. As already mentioned, Moser here was largely rejecting the German Symbolist climate. In his iconography he avails himself of a fantastical mythology and of a wedding between nature and the groups of fairies, undines, naiads, elves, and centaurs around which circle more decorative motifs and the Jugendstil. For the allegory of *Musik*, Moser arranges three nude crouching women, modeling them strongly with light and shadow in a bold graphic style that, as with the other allegories, is reminiscent of Klinger. Much later, from 1913 to 1915, Moser would invoke the allegorical theme of the three maidens in his *Drei kauerende Frauen*, but with an intensified symbolism. The *Allegorien*, nevertheless, provide an important reference point for the later graphic works for *Ver Sacrum* and for the Secession.

Relief for *Ver Sacrum* in copper, ca. 1900. (Collection J. Hummel, Vienna)

Moser also did illustrations for children's fairy tales published by Gerlach in the same period. He worked on the pamphlet *Für die Jugend des Volkes* (1894) and on the volumes titled *Bummelei* by Eduard Pötzl,[9] and on *Waidmannsheil* and *Jugendschatz deutscher Dichtung* by Felicie Ewarts.[10] In these publications the scenes are often composed in a style ranging from angular and sharp to subtle, focusing on the head and striving for a unitary effect. Above all, Moser concentrated on the figure used as a framing device or left free in decorative groups. Only from 1897 to 1898 did he display a more decisive awareness of two-dimensionality, surrounding masses with solids and voids, and contrasting negatives and positives, white and black. His flora and fauna—in particular, the butterfly—became more stylized, more imaginary, more abstract, and less traditional than those of the period.

Japonisme *in the West*

As already noted, European art at the turn of the century was significantly affected by influences from the Far East, particularly from Japan. The phenomenon was manifest in painting and major art forms, as well as in applied and decorative art. This is seen above all in graphics, from the French school of posters by Cheret, Toulouse-Lautrec, and Orazi, to the British tradition of book illustration from Beardsley to Voysey, to the American Bradley.

According to Siegfried Wichmann,[11] one of the most knowledgeable scholars of this phenomenon, *Japonisme* fundamentally affected the course of modern art in a variety of ways. From a technical standpoint, there arose a black-and-white graphic style that unquestionably derived from the style of the Oriental woodcut. In terms of content, there was a return to a symbolism involving natural forms, such as flowers and animals, and exotic subjects so typical

[9] A Robert Mohr publication.
[10] Published by von Waldheim, 1897.
[11] S. Wichmann, *Japonismus, Ostasien, Europa: Begegnungen in der Kunst des 19. und 20. Jahrhunderts*, Herrsching, Schuler Verlagsgesellschaft mbH, 1908.

Pattern study, 1899. (Collection J. Hummel, Vienna)

of Japanese culture. The human figure and other natural elements tended to be highly stylized, and even geometric decorations, including elements from calligraphy and ancient Japanese symbols, were often introduced into the composition. Seals, emblems, and elaborations on Oriental signs also gained much attention in Europe at the turn of the century. Certain configurations gained particular notoriety. Multiple forms interacting with one another (as with *Ver Sacrum*) and elongated forms introduced European artists to a new sense of order. Among the subjects preferred, besides a vast botanical repertoire and explicit references to entomology (especially by Gallé) were the figurative lexicon of the wave, with its strong representative suggestion; the carp; and other fish that served as symbols of vitality; as well as birds and butterflies.

In this way *Japonisme* affected all of European representative and decorative art as well as theater and ballet. By the turn of the century European art was thus on its way to becoming what we know as contemporary art. Art abandoned and rejected academic principles in order to embrace a new expression and iconography: academic realism and naturalism in art and symbolism were accordingly transformed.

It is important to stress that these incursions of Oriental art into Europe occurred at the major Western commercial gateways to Japan, particularly in Russia, England, and France around 1854. The universal exhibitions of the time therefore served as the echo if not as the sound box of what was happening. The intellectual and artistic activity of Samuel Bing, a noted art dealer, was of great importance. Bing, a German and the largest collector in Paris of Japanese prints and woodblocks prints, including numerous Utamaros, began selling Oriental art in 1888. In 1888 he also began to publish the journal *Japon Artistique* in French, German and English. In 1893 the Galerie Durant-Ruel, the most famous in Paris for its Impressionist paintings, exhibited an Utamaro by Hiroshige in a show organized by Bing. Arthur Lasenby Liberty, an English businessman, was energetically promoting the new Oriental aesthetic in London as well.

Thus Art Nouveau and Jugendstil surrendered to Japanese art, and a secular tradition that had been handed down with great respect through the generations was diffused throughout Europe and adopted by European artists.

Vienna was certainly an integral part of the spread of *Japonisme*. More than acting merely as a filter for Japanese art from other countries, as England and France did, Vienna demonstrated, according to Wichmann, that it had the artistic autonomy and cultural resources to assimilate the new aesthetic trends. "Around 1900, Japanese prints, particularly Katagami, gained even greater importance in European decorative art. In 1873, in fact, the Österreichisches Museum für Kunst und Industrie bought nearly 1,000 original Katagami prints for the World Exhibition. This abundance of material had a consistent effect on the contemporary art world, and the artists of the Secession in Vienna and of the Wiener Werkstätte were connoisseurs of Katagami. Like Josef Hoffmann, Kolo Moser and other artists all used Japanese designs as models."[12]

12 Ibid.

13

Klimt's pictorial work betrays the influence of the Japanese masters of the Uki-joe; over his compositions Klimt superimposed a stereotypic decoration, minute, and geometric, and he strove also for a two-dimensionality and a total elimination of volume.

These same characteristics are evident in Moser's work as well: it demonstrates a conspicuous use of typically Japanese styles, themes, and modes of representation. But Moser achieved this without falling prey to mere imitation. Inspired by the Japanese models, he transcended the strictly experimental level of art. In his use of the wave motif, for example, Moser transforms the Japanese motif for water into a personification, a concept of Western mythology. And like Klimt, Moser added to the recurrent symbolic motifs of Oriental art (flowers, plants, fish, birds, or geometric emblems) and imbued them with sensuality and an exalted feminine beauty.

Moser's references to Japanese art are numerous: in *Tunkpapiers*, a color stain technique; elongated figures (e.g., the poster for the XIII Secession of 1902, or the collages of 1904); the vignette for *Ver Sacrum*, 1898, 1, 11; compositional abstraction, as in the glass window for the Hotel Bristol in Warsaw; and figures synthesized into a mass of black, yet conveying two-dimensionality through the strong contour line (*Fromme Kalender*, 1898). These and other affinities with Japanese art can be seen in most of Moser's graphics. In addition to these formal and technical matters, he explored design problems: experimenting, for example, with the ambiguity of designs in which birds and fish are arranged in negative-positive relationships and reiterated in patterns or sequences.

Cover for *Ver Sacrum*, n. 4, 1899.

The Birth of Ver Sacrum

The journal *Ver Sacrum* commenced in January of 1898, and served as the official organ of the Vereinigung Bildender Künstler Österreichs-Secession. This organization was a movement of the Secession and was formed by two artistic groups, the Siebner Club and the Hagengesellschaft. In his autobiography Josef Hoffmann wrote that "we all sensed the birth of a new movement opening new paths to painting and sculpture. I was fascinated by a small group of artists at the Academy that jokingly called themselves 'The Club of Seven' (Siebner Club) who explored new forms of painting and sculpture. The painter Koloman Moser was the catalyst for this small group of forerunners. He was very demanding and never satisfied. In the course of our everyday contact with him, Moser sparked our interests in figurative art. We were attracted by the successful accomplishments of his graphic work."[13]

The decision to publish *Ver Sacrum* was reached at the first meeting of the Secessionists in 1897. The title, as Max Burckhard attests, was a reference to the "sacred spring" of Roman tradition. The first issue stated the aims of the group: to strive for the integration of art and the elimination of the barriers

[13] J. Hoffmann, "Selbstbiographie," 1950, published in *Ver Sacrum—Neue Folge*, 1972.

Illustration for *Ver Sacrum*, n. 11, 1898.

Girl with Roses, 1898. (Collection J. Hummel, Vienna)

[14] L. Hevesi, *Acht Jahre Sezession*.
[15] Complete description by G. Fannelli in *Il disegno Liberty*, Rome/Bari, Laterza, 1981.

that exist between "major and minor" art, and to reconcile art with the most advanced philosophical theories of art developed by Riegl and Fiedler. Contributions came not only from painters and architects of the group, such as Klimt, Olbrich, Hoffmann, and Moser, but also from men of letters and critics such as Ludwig Hevesi, Hermann Bahr, Max Burckhard, and the writers Hofmannsthal, Holz, Rilke, Bierbaum, and Maeterlinck.

Together with the Secessionhaus planned by Olbrich and the innovative spirit of the time, *Ver Sacrum* proposed a new program of artistic renewal. Exhibitions and publications created such a widespread interest that in 1898, after just over one year of activity, Hevesi wrote with great satisfaction, "All Vienna has become Secessionist."[14]

Thematically *Ver Sacrum* expressed the same ideals as the Secessionist movement: the same mythology and the distinction between the sacred and the profane; the ideals of urban life and the value of popular tradition (*Heimatkunst*); the metaphor of fable, the limits of magic and of mysticism.[15] Bahr and Burckhard formed a council to edit the work of the first year which was published by Gerlach & Schenk. The journal was then published by Seemann. Moser, Olbrich, Alfred Roller, and Friedrich König all took turns acting as editor-in-chief of *Ver Sacrum*. In keeping with the geometric ideals of its creators, the journal was issued in a rigorously square format, 29 by 29 centimeters.

Under an increasingly sophisticated graphic approach the pages of the journal became encased in a stylized two-dimensional design with numerous recurrent ornamental friezes, cornices, vignettes, and decorative vignettes. The compositions became quite complicated, especially those to which more than one artist contributed. The rigorous, symmetrical pagination left space for ample margins and illustrations. The illustrated plates ranged from spontaneous images drawn from the world of nature to those derived from the symbolic world. In some cases, the publication's symmetry derived from the idea of the mirror and therefore from the idea of the double image: a symbolist landscape reflected on the surface of a lake or pond.

Ver Sacrum met with immediate success. Two articles in the second year of the publication laid the groundwork for the great exhibition of Japanese art in 1900.

From 1900 on, *Ver Sacrum* changed from a monthly to a bimonthly magazine, attaining great stylistic continuity and graphic coherence. Some issues were monographic in treatment, others less thematic: Rilke, for example, contributed articles on Örlik, while Hevesi wrote on Hoffmann. During the fourth year of publication, separate issues were devoted to Klimt, Georges Minne, and Mackintosh. Increasingly the stylists imposed their personal styles on the graphic design of the pages. Especially characteristic were the curves and ornamental motifs arranged in insistently repetitive patterns. Benirschke designed trees in the form of concentric disks. Adolf Böhm wedded vegetable spirals with rectilinear axes. Ernst Stöhr, who was also a writer, made small abstract representations. The graphic designs of Klimt feature sensual, continuous lines; they are lighthearted compositions, without excessive contrasts but rich in symbolic allusions and references to an eclectic culture. Figures from classical Greece and Mediterranean mythology, and in particular from the myths of ancient Crete, combine with symbolism and cosmology and with other esoteric characteristics. The esoteric and symbolic aspects of occult initiation clearly emerge in some of the illustrations for *Ver Sacrum*, especially the calender designs by Friedrich König, Josef Maria Auchenthaller, and Wilhelm List. In other cases Klimt seemed to celebrate the "reconciliation between paganism and Christianity" in an era he considered illuminated. His *Theseus and the Minotaur* was the poster for the first Secession exhibition in 1897. In general, his themes in *Ver Sacrum* are the same as those in his paintings: the reflection of contemporary values, the cyclic conceptions of man, nature, and the cosmos where, as Alessandra Comini wrote, "this existence is based on one single principle of fertility and regeneration."[16] Another recurrent idea is that of Nietzsche's "eternal return"—a symbolic vision of the world, entirely permeated by sensuality and eroticism.

Otto Czeschka, with his increasingly Byzantine decorative style, expressed another aspect of the Wienerstil. His many decorations, including metal relief panels, book covers, and—among his most noted graphic works—illustrations for the *Nibelungen*, were all executed with a Japanese flavor. The prints and illustrations by Alfred Roller, a celebrated Viennese set designer, were closer in character to the continental taste of Art Nouveau of Franco-Belgian origin.

Kolo Moser also found self-expression through a symbolist conception. As with Klimt, Moser communicated his message through mythical and spiritual figures: muses, heralds, and angels. Although only six years Klimt's junior, Moser progressed rapidly, transcending the Symbolist influences from Munich in order to align himself with the younger generation of artists such as Egon Schiele, Oskar Kokoschka, and Berthold Löffler. Upon the images of the classical past he began to superimpose elements of the psyche and of Gestalt theory. His style, therefore, was not consistent: in some cases he used a continuous, flexible line, while in other cases he would delineate form by contrasting white and black masses. Elsewhere his compositions were rigidly geometric, and would involve the human figure in their shapes. In many cases he would cut down the composition to achieve a close-up and to give emphasis to the subject. Moser preferred to experiment. He was an eclectic illustrator with no fear of incoherence; in fact, he loved variety and innovation. Reflecting this exuberance and versatility, his works virtually explode in a display of pyrotechnic virtuosity. Stylized Art Nouveau figures mix with a more abstract style involving squares, rhomboids, and triangles. In the eighteenth installment there is an interesting woodcut experiment: the block is pressed onto paper without any ink, making the image in relief visible only under a very close light.

Many artists made contributions to *Ver Sacrum*. Roller designed the first cover with its symbolic force—the roots of a sapling breaking through the vase that holds it, a reference to the creative forces of the Secession. König, Czeschka,

16 A. Comini, *Gustav Klimt*, New York, Braziller, 1975.

Book cover for *Jugendschatz Deutscher Dichtungen*, 1897. (Hochschule für Angewandte Kunst, Vienna)

Leopold Stolba, Maximilian Kurzweil, Maximilian Lenz, List, and Ferdinand Andri also contributed. The most notable characteristic of *Ver Sacrum* was that it combined the contributions of painters and architects from diverse backgrounds. The furniture designs of Moser and Hoffmann done in the journal's fifth year (1902) are featured in photographs of the time. And the twelfth issue of that year is entirely devoted to Max Klinger's statue *Beethoven*, to Klimt's *Beethoven Frieze* and to the exhibition dedicated to Hoffmann.

The Geometric as a Counter to Figural Sensuality

The terms *ornament* and *decoration* are used here with more than their usual meanings in artistic terminology—in addition to their traditional niches in the artistic lexicon they also refer to the psychology of pictorial representation, the integration of architectonic elements, the enrichment of utilitarian objects, or the structuring of graphic work. After the time when so much decoration was understood as a copy of past styles—such as Neoclassicism, eclecticism, and the Neo-Gothic—an autonomous decorative consciousness came into being that, although it derived from the observation of nature, availed itself of a much fuller visual culture. Along with Japanese influences, a concept of the geometric was also introduced. The revolution in design taking place in mid-nineteenth-century England among such artists as Augustus Welby Pugin, William Morris, Owen Jones, and Walter Crane took full cognizance of the new ornamental tendencies that would eventually lead to Art Nouveau. Owen Jones's *The Grammar of Ornament*, published in 1856, was considered the classical text, influencing all types of ornamental design and serving as the source for all successive studies. Jones wrote about the "melody of form," the harmony of line, of quietude and equilibrium. But this "quietude" is not to be confused with simplicity. According to Jones, all moldings and decorations are based on curves of superior order, as with a conic section, while in decadent art, circles and curves produced by the compass predominate.[17] To a great extent, the reforms in modern decorative art are due to the new "grammar" formulated by Jones.

The notion that ornament had a purely "artistic value," or that it was a "crime," lingered long among such eminent critics, philosophers, architects, and artists as John Ruskin, Ralph Wornum, Gottfried Semper, and Adolf Loos. Loos, adopting a radically extreme position, accepted ornament only as an expression of primitive art, and thus separated it from cultivated art. He responded to the work of Austrian designers with his *Ornament und Verbrechen* (1908). The process of the simplification of form, however, was already taking place. Mackintosh, Hoffmann, and Moser had already completed a circle, a structural parabola of geometric origin. The divorce between the functions of art and of design would be accepted only by a later generation. Gombrich wrote that "not only did it become an article of faith that the ornamentation of houses,

[17] O. Jones, *The Grammar of Ornament*, London, 1856.

furnishings, and household goods was fundamentally in poor taste, it was also admitted that the formal imagination which had thus lost its traditional outlet had to be given a new field of action. It was in the period when the creation of decorative forms was increasingly suppressed in favor of functional utility that what is called abstract art made its entrance into the presence of painting and sculpture."[18] Gombrich also noted that the exigencies of functionalism threatened to lead to the ultimate death of ornament, whereby elaborate patterns would be transformed into "abstract art."[19] It must not be forgotten that the fundamentals of modern basic design and of Gestalt theory are based on Moser's ornamental formulation.

It is valid to say, therefore, that a new consciousness came into being in the 1890s in both architecture and decorative art—a search into the structure of form that was no longer bound to the styles of the past, but rather to an internal search, either of an organic or of a more geometric and abstract nature. Above all, the line became a principal syntactical element, a potent means of expression and abstraction.

The theoretical studies of Walter Crane after 1888, concluding with *Line and Form* in 1900, are of great didactic significance. For Crane, line was more important than anything else. Delicate, emphatic, expressive line—which controls and unifies all—is the basis of all rendering.[20] According to Crane, line can also assume a symbolic function. Inherent in line is a process of simplification, a clear tendency toward abstraction.

Line and Form supplied the guidelines for all designers at the turn of the century. Among its subjects were the origin and function of contour lines, the language of line in both representational and ornamental design, the choice and use of line, the choice of form from elementary shapes to the derivation of decorative patterns from squares and circles, and the principles of structural and decorative line in organic forms. Crane also made a distinction between descriptive and decorative (two-dimensional) solutions to artistic problems. English artists and designers of the Arts and Crafts movement tended toward space-filling decoration, and some, such as Charles Annesley Voysey and Arthur Heygate Mackmurdo, achieved remarkable results with this practice.

As already remarked, the example set by English designers had great repercussions throughout Europe in the early 1890s. In *Stilfragen* (1893) the Austrian Alois Riegl revealed the fundamental nature of ornament through a study of the minor arts in a diverse range of ancient cultures. Kolo Moser came into contact with Mackintosh, Khnopff, Klinger, and Crane, and, like other Viennese artists, he studied particular aspects of Japanese art and deepened his studied of line and form in Western art. This led rapidly to an emphasis on geometry. The print and frieze designs bear witness to this evolution, for example, in the double pages for Rilke in *Ver Sacrum* ("Vorführung," 1901), with its kinetic chessboard pattern, in the stamps and book bindings, as in the cover for the monograph on Segantini (1902), and for the Kohn Company logo. This is also evident in the decoration for furnishings and jewelry. His posters were

Study for stamp commemorating the Emperor's Jubilee, 1908. (Private Collection, Vienna)

[18] E. Gombrich, *The Sense of Order: A Study in the Psychology of Decorative Art*, Oxford, Phaidon Press, 1979.
[19] Ibid.
[20] W. Crane, *Line and Form*, London, 1900.

Advertisement vignette for Theyer & Hardmuth for *Ver Sacrum*, ca. 1899. (Private Collection, Vienna)

promptly recorded in the pages of *Die Fläche*, a graphics publication printed with great care using the technique of chromolithography. The commemorative volume *Die K.K. Hof-und Staatsdruckerei 1804-1904*, with wood engravings by Czeschka, borders by Moser, and typography by Larish, is of special interest. The inspiration for the work was derived from the schemes in Morris's Kelmscott Press. Typography was also used for the various publications concerning the Imperial Jubilee of 1908. Moser cared for the major part of this. Applied graphics was of particular relevance to Art Nouveau production, and many Art Nouveau artists, including Behrens, Eckmann, Bradley, van de Velde, and Moser, also studied typographic characters. In Vienna, the typographic character was almost always valued as a decorative element, as a means of lending harmony and unity to the design. The work of artists from Klimt to Löffler attests to this, and Moser was the supreme master of its use.

The progressive accentuation of geometry and of mastery of the use of line made apparent the importance that design instruction held for the Secessionists. As Fanelli remarks in his *Il disegno Liberty*, "From 1899 onward, Moser, Roller, Hoffmann, Cizek, and von Larisch introduced to the Kunstgewerbeschule a complete turnaround of tradition, emphasizing the general study of the structure of form... One operating component of this process was a geometry of intuitive nature—elementary, unscientific, assimilated solely through the Japanese artistic process; another factor was a detailed transformation of traditional Western geometry, reinterpreted as instrument of identification of abstract forms in the natural variety, therefore coinciding with the first element, but also as influence of the theories of pure visibility."[21]

Pattern as the Basis for a New Mode of Visualization

A sense of order is considered by many to be a peculiarly human trait. The concept of a mode of vision that is ordered and based on a geometry of form finds its purest expression in ancient Greece in the geometry of Euclid and the thought of Plato. This quest for a sublime order intensified in the Renaissance and in all subsequent forms of classicism and academicism. Modern man, however, increasingly identifies with the artificial Cartesian order which views the world in an entirely different way. According to Ernst Gombrich, so profound and intrinsic is our tendency to look for order that we instinctively react every time we perceive regularity in the natural world.[22]

Beyond the new "classicism" that has been achieved through symmetry, research into the processes of abstraction in art have led to new visual phenomena and perceptions closely connected with graphic representation. Scientific theories have been anticipated by the artist's search for negative form, the reiteration of form, and the new figure-background relationship.

Since 1890 the Austrian philosopher von Ehrenfelds had affirmed the independence of the "quality of form" from its constitutive elements. But it is

21 G. Fanelli.
22 E. Gombrich.

unlikely that Moser would have been aware of these writings. More probably he—like van de Velde—had a greater predisposition to theorizing and a marked interest in the aesthetics of *Einfühlung*. Already in 1897, in fact, van de Velde had written in *Pan*: "Maximum equilibrium or spiritual clarity will be made possible only through a quest for aesthetic value that belongs not only to the positive but also to the negative outline of the object, and this, perhaps, constitutes the most valuable aspect of our discovery. I mean that the perception of each piece of furniture, each object, besides its own profile that defines it from the wall or surrounding space, in short, in each type of background, another form is delineated which is equal and contrary that adapts perfectly to the shape. This negative form is just as important as that of the object itself and makes possible a secure means of assessing its beauty."[23]

Moreover, van de Velde theorized about a line force and, in opposition to all passive naturalism, maintained that "the line derives energy from the outline it traces."[24] At the same time, as already noted, observations about the two-dimensionality of ornamental design, on the contours of its configuration, on the equilibrium between positive and negative, in short on the visual speculation that design produces, formed part of various theoretical ideas. Again, in Austria, A. Hölzel published an article in *Ver Sacrum* in which he made note of the changes and different visual effects that various elements, seen as pure form, assume in the landscape. The attempt here was to overcome the customary limits of empiricism.

Von Larisch, on the other hand, constructed a didactic method based on the reversibility of the graphic sign: the ornament and typographic character are viewed as the negative of the background. Up to this time the background had no ornamental characteristics whatsoever. The figures and background had entered into a relationship of connection and alternative. These visual studies were expanded and explored more deeply at the turn of the century, and the so-called Berlin School came into being and utilized Gestalt theory.

Douat's *Method of Permutation*, written in 1704, constitutes the very first treatise on design theory as it relates to symmetrical composition. This is an analytic method for a series of patterns generated ad infinitum from diagonally subdivided squares, which yielded black and white triangles. It is a real electrical program nearly three centuries old. Persian and Peruvian carpet design is another example of geometric coding and pattern.

Kolo Moser had not written any treatises or theories on such visual phenomena; he chose instead a more pragmatic route, a poetic route of sublimated representation. He frequently transformed figures into abstract shapes, producing mere ciphers completely divorced from naturalistic representation. Gombrich referred to this invention of Moser's as counterchange. This repetition of the figure in positive and negative leads to a perceived reversibility. The so-called Rich Catch of Fish of 1899 is a good example of this, and the Japanese influence is clearly evident in the treatment of black and white masses and the unitary effect achieved by the composition.

[23] H. van de Velde, in *Pan*, 1897.
[24] H. van de Velde, in *Zum neuen Stil aus seinen Schriften ausgewählt and eingeleitet*, Munich, 1955.

Fabric design, published in *Ver Sacrum*, n. 4, 1899.

Such patterns are characteristic of the fabric patterns (*gewebter Flächenschmuck*) designed by Moser between 1899 and 1900 and produced by Backhausen. Their greatest expression, however, is to be found in the thirty plates Moser designed for the fabric and wallpaper catalogue that Gerlach published in 1902. Titled *Flächenschmuck*, this was the third volume of the series *Die Quelle*. The decorative motifs were derived from the animal, vegetable, and human realms, and remained strongly two-dimensional, forming interconnecting structures in which the negative-positive contrasts blended into refined patterns of color. According to Gombrich, "counterchange, the correspondence between positive and negative shapes, is certainly in its origin the simple consequence of commonplace technical procedures. It will emerge in matting or basket work whenever two varieties of cane or leaves are used to create nothing more surprising than a checkerboard pattern or a Greek fretwork. The correspondence thus created must have appealed to decorators all over the world. It occurs among the pattern of Amazon Indians and in a more complex form in ancient Mexico. But the supreme masters of counterchange were no doubt the Islamic designers who modified their grid patterns until figure and void corresponded in the most surprising way. To achieve this kind of correspondence the designer must again use the step-by-step method of 'Graded Complication.' There must always be a give and take in the modification of the figure and the background."[25]

The image of interlocking figures in a potentially infinite pattern of repetition is a kind of visual joke that modifies the figure, and frequently produces undesirable results. The Victorian writer Lewis F. Day, in fact, in his 1890 manual on wallpaper, spoke of the risk of a design failing or losing its standard quality, and consequently recommended the use of diagonal rather than horizontal designs.[26]

Moser elaborated on his earlier experience with Katagami by using Japanese masks for a pattern printed on fabrics in a complex composition of rigorous order and rhythm. Already in April 1899 Moser had published a series of *Flächenmusters* (fabric, wallpaper, and carpet design) in *Ver Sacrum*. These were made into pages as decorative motifs to be integrated into the text. This also bears the unmistakable influence of Katagami, and moreover, anticipates by two years the plates of the *Flächenschmuck* of the *Die Quelle* series published by Gerlach, in which Moser used the same system by Katagami.

The plates display a gradual trend toward greater stylization, going from stylized figures to geometric abstraction. The sixty compositions (thirty on the front, thirty on the reverse side), include four derived from the kaleidoscope, fourteen stylized vegetable compositions, three geometric shapes, one of mermaids and angels, one of fish, one of butterflies, two of birds, two of organic and inorganic geometric forms, and seven of purely geometric shapes.

This collection of works displays such a great mastery of expression, geometric elaboration of figurative and organic motifs, chromatic interpretations, use of typographic characters, references to Oriental emblems, and kaleidoscopic fan-

[25] E. Gombrich.
[26] L.F. Day, *Ornamental Design*, London, 1890, cited in E. Gombrich.

tansies that Kolo Moser may rightly be considered as one of the founding fathers of modern graphic art.

The Glass Window: Light and Structure

The gilded cupola of the church of St. Leopold am Steinhof, designed by Otto Wagner and erected in 1904, tops the Viennese psychiatric hospital at the summit of the Baumgartner Höhe. Considered as a retreat from the chromatic tones of the Secessionists, the white and gold of the church surrounded by the fields of green appeared to evoke a "melancholy joy."[27] The subtle grid of symmetrical lines on the outside of the cupola is played off by sharp lines of the marble masonry. Above the entrance, four bronze angels standing directly over an aedicula have semicircular glass wings designed by Kolo Moser.

"The throne of the Father stood in the center, and on either side two angels clad in costly vestments and with superb open wings. In the far corner knelt Adam and Eve, placed almost at the trailing of large curving plants. The light that shone through this window and two others in the transept was transformed into white and gold, green and blue. In the transept windows also, large angelic figures appeared in all their glory. Two angels in the upper semicircular area of the window, suspended above the saints who depicted the acts of mercy, had magnificent peacock wings. Moser also designed two angels for the great altar constructed of majolica, stucco and mosaic. These angels stood in a frontal position and held signs of the martyrdom of Christ. The principal panel in the center illustrated the triumph of Christ amid a choir of saints, including the protectress Dymphna."[28]

For the interior of the church Wagner wanted to achieve the maximum luminosity possible, and therefore he avoided excessively coloristic and figured effects. Accordingly, the walls were plastered in white and supplied with a three-meter-high white marble socle. The floor consisted of a black and white mosaic. Chandeliers were fashioned out of gilded metal and blue glass, and furnishings were of dark oak. The altar, also dressed in marble and gold, was covered by a cupola in gilded metal adorned with blue stones and small enamel heads of angels. For Wagner, this was to be the central focus of the interior. The upper part with Moser's mosaic was finished in stucco, white below, the figures would have had vestments in light and dark-colored marble, polychrome heads and hands, and gilded metal for halos and other details. Inserted into all of this was a profusion of glass mosaic, mother-of-pearl, and cut stones.

In the autumn of 1904 Moser made designs for the large window over the entrance with the intention of emphasizing the figured effect of the exterior and of producing a magical source of light for the interior by means of glass windows. "The project was commissioned by a group of representatives from the area, the church and the architect. The church official objected to the plans. So a commission member and the architect sought the approval of another ec-

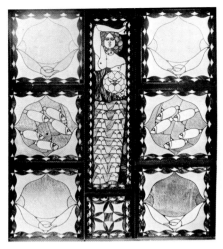

Glass panels for window, ca. 1904.

[27] J.A. Lux, speaking in 1914 about the "blessed joy" at the sight of the church.
[28] M. Cacciari, *Dallo Steinhof: Prospettive viennesi del primo '900*, Milan, Adelphi, 1980.

Pattern study, 1899. (Collection J. Hummel, Vienna)

clesiastical member who would not object to the plans. In spring the side windows were completed for the wall around the main altar. The first plans for the decoration of the altar were immediately rejected despite the fact that apparently a personality of high artistic sensibility representing the church was to blame."[29]

Understandably, from this time on the cordial rapport that Moser and Wagner had enjoyed with the ecclesiastical authorities began to break down irreversibly, eventually ending in legal action and a trial. Because of these external complications the work remained only partially complete. In the narrow-minded view of the church representative, Moser was unsuited to design a decorative program for the church because of his Protestant background. Certainly, the aura of the church of St. Leopold cannot be described as profoundly mystical, but this is true of all kinds of Italian paintings of the fifteenth and sixteenth centuries, such as those of Benozzo Gozzoli or Gentile da Fabriano. The thick lead latticework of the stained glass windows weakened the structural effectiveness of the art, rendering it static and mannered. The high level of quality that may be seen in Moser's Steinhof mosaics and windows is missing: Moser seems to be prisoner of an elegant formalism that limited his typical creative exuberance.

Moser displayed a surprising versatility in working with many different media. There is a high degree of technical competency in his works in glass. More than an artistic sensibility, one senses in Moser a true mastery and craftsmanship that allow him to overcome all obstacles. He undertook the glass window theme in 1898 for the inside of the Secession palace, and in 1900, in collaboration with Wagner, completed a window for the Apollo firm and one for the Lederer House. In 1901 he designed a large window composition representing four female figures in an abstract landscape for the Hotel Bristol in Warsaw. Despite the unfortunate experience with the Steinhof church, Moser participated in a competition to create pictorial decoration for the Santo Spirito church in Düsseldorf—and won. This work foresees the decoration of the presbytery, the great altar, side altars, and central nave that Moser completed with a rich decoration in Neo-Byzantine style. Considering the polemical nature of the competition, Moser viewed his Düsseldorf project as an exception. "The official conditions gave the artist full liberty... I decided to try religious subject matter that would be confronted and resolved without spiritual counsel."[30] Even though his project was never realized, Moser's plans won admiration at an exhibition of Christian art held in Düsseldorf in 1909.

[29] K. Moser, in *Deutsche Kunst und Dekoration*, n. 21, 1907-08.
[30] From *Mein Werdegang*, and also included in W. Schweiger, *Vom Schreibtisch und aus dem Atelier*.
[31] K. Moser, "Bühnenbilder und Kostüm-Entwürfe zu 'Der Musikant'," in *Deutsche Kunst und Dekoration*, n. 27, 1910-11.

Art for the Theater

"In performance of a dramatic opera it is the events themselves that create the scenography."[31] Thus said Kolo Moser, speaking of scenography and costumes for Julius Bittner's *Der Musikant*, performed at the Hofoper in 1910-1911. "Besides the events of the scene," continues Moser, "form, color and light create the scenography."[32] This was an abstract, conceptual vision of the theater, which he applied as part of his reform of the Viennese theater. "It is not the motif literally copied from nature, but rather that which is absolutely indispensable for the opera that gives credibility to the scenography. Naturalism can increase verisimilitude without being necessary for this... A backdrop painted with trees gives the spectator the idea of a forest, although in reality the trees should appear in the distance and have depth instead of being all on one plane as on the backdrop. Now place a bench in front of the backdrop. Immediately the woods that I first 'saw' with imagination now become a mere flat painting when seen in conjunction with the three-dimensional bench. But by placing more trees behind or to the side of the backdrop, a new illusion of a forest with depth is achieved. In the very same way, an actor placed in front of a painted backdrop gives the impression of a silhouette."[33]

Moser's theories about the theater had an impact not on the idea of illusion, but on realism. Today, his ideas may seem an accepted means of expression, but in Moser's time the situation was more delicate. Moser's collaboration with the author Felix Salten in 1901 for the experimental theater at the Jung-Wiener Theater zum lieben Augustin could be considered the first truly experimental theater in Vienna. The set was based on a circular background of fabric subdivided only by geometrical ornament. Similar hangings also covered the interior walls. This was, indeed, a courageous choice on the road to pure abstraction.

As is well known, Vienna was noted for its prestigious theater, a kind of royal theater distinguished for the concepts it represented and for its scenographic architecture. At the turn of the century in Vienna the theater was certainly the least revolutionary of all the arts. Schnitzler, Hofmannsthal, Bahr, and Salten all had to go to Berlin or Dresden for the premieres of their works. The staging of new theatrical works in Vienna, at least in the first decade of this century, always met with utter failure.

Only in musical theater was innovation of any kind accepted. Here the collaboration of Gustav Mahler, the director of the Hofoper, and Alfred Roller, who was responsible for scenic adaptation, soon led to rapid, vigorous reform. With their high professionalism, Mahler and Roller sought to make the ideal of opera as a universal art a reality, striving to liberate the stage from the burden of realism in order to achieve a more fluid and allusive atmosphere. At the start of the century, however, Salten's theater did not enjoy success with either conservative critics or more radical personalities such as Karl Kraus, who deemed Moser's scenic backdrops totally deleterious. The origins of this kind of theater lay in the "*mise-en-scène* movement" developed by Hermann Bahr and his colleagues. Bahr was in favor of the first performances without denying the controversies that would arise: "Hearty applause, box office success, fanatical enthusiasm, pernicious exasperation, a real battle among the members... Moser

Figure study, ca. 1910. (Private Collection, Vienna)

[32] Ibid.
[33] Ibid. Also published in W. Schweiger, *Vom Schreibtisch und aus dem Atelier.*

Costumes for *Der Musikant* by Julius Bittner, 1910-11. (From *Deutsche Kunst und Dekoration*, n. 27, 1910-11)

has composed a charming little space of great simplicity—only a white curtain and a pair of delicate lines of ornament."[34] It was Bahr as well who, several years later, gave his support to the experimental staging that had been initiated by Olbrich at Darmstadt and was immediately continued by Moser in his work with Salten.

The new theatrical formulae that completely overturned the old schematics can be seen in the stage design for the Cabaret Fledermaus in 1907, conceived under the influence of Hoffmann. The goal here was to create a setting which would provoke "a feeling of an elevated style of life and initiate an authentic culture of diversion. This theater-cellar was a typical expression of the Secession in its final stage, with rigorous lines, and decoration that was elegant, bold, and spirited."[35] Among the collaborators was Peter Altenberg, who composed the prologue for the premiere, and Hermann Bahr, Richard Dehmel, Robert Musil and Detlev Liliencron. In the first season of 1907-1908 Moser collaborated at the Fledermaus to create dance costumes for Gertrude Barrison. Peter Altenberg commented that the dancer resembled a novel, long-forgotted species of bird.[36] Commenting on the costumes that Moser designed in 1909 for Brattie Young and Nelly Moyse for *Die Fledermaus*, Altenberg wrote: "Kolo Moser has designed black and white costumes that are completely original, with a kind of drapery heretofore nonexistent—an attire both masculine and feminine at the same time."[37] In Moser's work we see manifest, evidently, the latest tendencies of the Wiener Werkstätte.

Also emanating from the Fledermaus theater was the Kunstschau theater. The pantomime *Die Tänzerin und die Marionette* by Max Mell was performed "on a stage of the greatest stylization, produced by E.J. Wimmer, with luminous white drapery suspended from the dark green of the trees." The greatest provocation for Vienna, however, came from Oskar Kokoschka's *Mörder, Hoffnung der Frauen* (Murder, Hope of Women) in 1909.

Theater from this point on was fundamentally transformed, but everything remained on an experimental level. Hermann Bahr said of this: "We have practically everything we need to create the best theater in the world—all we lack are followers. It is not a leader that we need: just someone clever enough to pass judgment on the painters."[38]

[34] H. Bahr, *Tagebuch*.
[35] W. Greissenegger, "L'arte scenica," in *Le arti a Vienna—Dalla Secessione alla caduta dell'impero asburgico*, Venice/Milan, Mazzotta, 1984.
[36] P. Altenberg, in *Wiener Allgemeiner Zeitung*, 26 January 1909.
[37] P. Altenberg, cited in K. Moser, *Mein Werdegang*.
[38] W. Greissenegger.
[39] W. Fenz, *Kolo Moser*, Salzburg/Vienna, Residenz Verlag, 1976.

Painting: From Realism to Cosmic Symbolism

Moser's activity as a painter was erratic. Despite the fact that he dedicated the last decade of his life almost exclusively to painting, the value of his work is not clear and his paintings are held in less esteem than his other artistic works. According to Werner Fenz, many of Moser's paintings, especially the early work, can be termed "insecure," and this is due in part to Moser's own self-criticism.[39]

Moser's early works are tied to a realist and academic tradition reflecting his training. Toward the end of the 1880s Moser attended a special class for historical painting taught by Mathias von Trenkwalt at the Academy for Figural Art. He painted the *Fairy Tales* (1891) at this time, a typically Viennese subject for the late nineteenth century with thematic references to the Biedermeier period. From the time of the commencement of the publication *Ver Sacrum* to the activity of the Werkstätte, Moser produced nothing of any fame. He did, however, develop a more luminous palette thanks to the influence of Moll and his circle. In fact, Moser adopted, as did Karl Moll, the objective language of Impressionism toward the turn of the century. His graphic works could bear comparison even to those of Klimt, for in their ideas, invention, decoration, and elegance and refinement, Moser sought a more lucid rapport with nature, one without any cerebral interference.

Love, ca. 1906. (Collection J. Hummel, Vienna)

The external tendencies of the Secession were numerous, from the Cézanne-like structure of the landscape to the chromaticism of the Munich Expressionists. For example, in Moser's painting all references to *Japonisme* disappeared and the minimal influences of the Greek and Byzantine elements in Klimt's art are missing. The refined atmosphere emerging from the Secessionist climate is not at all evident in the mythological paintings before 1907, unlike the presence of the symbolic synthesis of Germanic origin.

Werner Hofmann wrote that "Kolo Moser is an example of a Secessionist artist with multiple possibilities. His versatility, however, may also indicate a degree of indecision. In his decorative designs there is in the beginning an element of eurythmics in the way he handles line: this gradually gives way to geometric design."[40] This transformation of the organic world by means of geometric lines reached its culmination in Moser's posters. The particular way in which Moser inserted the human form into a flat, abstract design (*Ver Sacrum*, 1901, no. 20) seems to foreshadow a characteristic feature of Klimt's work a few years later.

Also apparent in Moser's work is the symbolism of his Swiss colleague Ferdinand Hodler, and to some extent the Norwegian Munch. In fact, Hodler's works appeared in an exhibition of the Secession prepared by Moser in 1904. Being Swiss, Hodler belonged to a culture greatly removed from that of centralized Germany. His paintings are accordingly forcefully personal, rude, and synthetic—the expression of a great artist removed from urban existence. Félix Vallotton spoke of him with great admiration and esteem. "His roughly executed art is highly masculine even when he tries to refine it and be graceful... Hodler is a poet of strength and struggle. His paintings aren't designed to please but to strike like a stone hurled from a catapult." As a painter under the influence of Hodler, Moser gave more incisive treatment to tapering lines without sacrificing eurythmics. If he eschews contours, as in certain depictions of clouds, Moser involves himself in an intermediate world in which color draws attention to certain objects, which nevertheless are imbued with their own power. In this case the clouds could transform themselves into a mountain range.

Study of vignette for *Ver Sacrum*, 1899. (Hochschule für angewandte Kunst, Vienna)

[40] W. Hoffmann, "La linea e il colore come espressione di sentimenti e sensazioni (secessioni, espressionismo, fauvismo)," in *L'arte moderna*, Milan, Fabbri, 1967.

Portrait of a Woman, oil on canvas, 1890-92. (Private Collection, Vienna)

The theoretical reflections of Hölzel also had a decisive influence on Moser's painting. In his article entitled "On Forms and the Distribution of Mass in the Composition" Hölzel spoke about the "schematic expression for planes transformed for nature studies, avoiding however tapering curves and repeated geometric design, characteristics encountered in versions rendered in completely different style."

With his exit from the Wiener Werkstätte, especially after 1907, Moser began to utilize the experience he had gained in his graphic art, gradually gravitating toward the artistic expression of Hodler without achieving the Swiss artist's harshness of expression. The year 1907 was one of transition for Moser, leading as it did to a more defined pictorial language. Moser refuted the plasticity of forms surrounded by a contour line. One phase of this development is apparent in the painting *Study of Semmering*, completed in 1907. A new degree of autonomy is reached with Moser's *Study of Fruit*, where again the Secession ideal of chromatic development is evident. The colored contour of the figure is important, a figure which has been rendered into a two-dimensional form on a flat panel, and therefore transformed into an unreal symbolic object.

Moser's work after 1913 displays a synthetic symbolism that culminated in the fixation of figural gestures and a deepening of the problems posed by the complementarity of color. He wrote about the issue of plane/depth and on color, on how to avoid the illusion of the stage on a panel and how to resolve parts of a shadow with specific colors. "The Semmering landscape of 1913 is transformed: the massiveness of the mountains is diminished and both colors and composition are muted."[41] In addition to naturalistic themes, Moser took to painting allegories in 1913 and 1914, as Hodler did also. These paintings are characterized by symbolic forms behind which silent figures move among clouds and nebulous bushes. Examples of this phase include *Das Licht* (Light), *Drei kauernde Frauen* (Three Crouching Women in a Landscape), *Venus in der Grotte* (Venus in a Grotto), *Liebestrank* (Pleasure of Love, 1915), and *Faust*.

In the painting *Das Licht* "a young man with a torch parts the clouds and drives off two airborne female figures. In Moser's work these clouds furnish color and depth, transferring the depiction from the real world to one with neither depth nor time."[42] By this time color constituted one of the prime elements in Moser's painting, and with it he achieved psychological effects, joking around with complementary features. In his *Wanderer* (The Wayfarer) a nude man with a staff vigorously treads across the clouds and trees, his body harmoniously situated in the panel, and his luminous profile enlivening the entire composition.

Moser made several studies on the same theme, using both chromatic and formal variations. The last one, his own self-portrait (1916), frontal with a bare chest, reveals his fixation on the face and his obsession with plasticity. The portrait's peasant contours and mysterious, mystical pose are characteristic of Moser's use of symbolism. His image seems overly enigmatic, an effect that foreshadowed his end. Two years after his death Moser was characterized in

Homage to the American Dancer, Loie Fuller, ca. 1900. (Graphische Sammlung Albertina, Vienna).

41 W. Fenz.
42 Ibid.

this way by his faithful friend Hermann Bahr: "Kolo Moser is dead. His countrymen viewed him as a stranger, and thus he died like one. Little by little he withdrew into silence, becoming distant even from the last of his few friends. Who he really was will thus remain hidden..."[43]

[43] Address delivered on the occasion of the first Moser retrospective in 1920; also included in *Tagebuch 1918*.

Moser Designer

Antonio D'Auria

Above: Graphics for stationery letterhead for the Wiener Werkstätte, 1904.

[1] H. Bahr, *Tagebuch 1918*, Innsbruck/Vienna/Munich, 1919, p. 163.
[2] K. Moser, *Mein Werdegang* (1916-17), in *Kolo Moser*, exhibition catalog edited by O. Oberhuber and J. Hummel, Vienna, 1979, p. 9.
[3] H. Focillon, *Vie des formes*, Paris, 1934, p. 18; cited in E. Gombrich, *The Sense of Order: A Study in the Psychology of Decorative Art* (Oxford: Phaidon Press, 1979).

Moser's Sense of Space

Nothing, says Amiel, is as successful as success. There's a point, in fact, where success functions like "vis inertiae," a sort of provident viscosity. The rise and fall of the Viennese Koloman Moser—from the height of the Wiener Werkstätte's activity to its gradual waning, which threatened Moser's work with oblivion—seems a testimonial to the fact that the public's acclaim must sometimes be questioned. The work's hope, on the contrary, is predicated on tragic uncertainty that only *time* can vindicate. It is pertinent to recall that this was the exact inverse of the trajectory that Loos's career followed.

Through his incredible concentration of intelligence, Moser was conscious, moreover, of paying the price of the social as well as the material success that he experienced in the dynamic clashing of opposing forces. It is undeniable that from the unique Moserian psychology—a mixture of resignation (as Bahr points out)[1] and a fascinating capacity for irony and realism—sprang an artistic production created by at least two sources of tension. On the one hand there was Moser's manual dexterity, which came from his precocious frequentation of the world of artisans;[2] and on the other, within him, there was an active, very precise underlying idea about the role of the client. Thus, as we shall see, his formal control was a dual one.

"Different styles," has Focillon written, "may exist at the same time, even in close adjacency."[3] Moser, artisan *sui generis* tangibly following the internal logic that governs forms, placed much value on the unencumbered clarity of Modernism. This may be seen, for example, in the wall arrangement in "Frau Dr. M.'s" dressing room, executed in Vienna around 1903, or the tomb of Saul Fineles in Vienna's central cemetery, in the same year; or in the armchair shown in the first exhibition of the Werkstätte in Berlin, 1904, designed probably with Hoffmann, or in the living room furniture of the Stonborough-Wittgenstein House in Berlin the following year.

On the other hand, in designing graphic fantasies and shadow rituals on ebony or mother-of-pearl Moser reinforced the bourgeois interior under the spoils of the precious, in the dream of the ubiquitous and determinant pattern. This is the way, then, that the "endless ornament," to use Fanelli's happy definition,[4] gives a unity and order to objects and their context. But it's not a matter of Horta's or Guimard's historical *horror vacui*, but certainly of something milder and "organized"; how often the search for a compositional ratio recalls one of the so-called fathers of rationalism, Otto Wagner. Like the Tafelflächen modules of the Karlsplatz station that conjugated the representational principles (the connotative element) with the avant-garde constructivist processes (loom structure with curtain panels), the Moserian ornamental patterns construct a compositional and perceptual model, thus providing a visual *order* in opposition to the Makart style, that "in its mixed odds and ends of the authentic and the false, "as van de Velde described it, "with its nightmarish invasion of whitewash," had invaded the bourgeois interiors.[5]

The point of convergence for these two opposing formal views, one just recently described as on its way to extinction and the other on the verge of being born, is constituted in Moser's idea of the Room. Under the guidance of Mackintosh's Scottish model, which favors the Room system over the articulation of the house as a whole,[6] Moser pushed the autonomy of each interior to the maximum. The unity is given or mimicked (if at all) by the recurrence of a motif, a frieze that rhymes and windingly articulates a space that is at times fluted and complex." Too many lives are needed to make a single one" seems to be the significance of a work in which all the effects are as excessive as in the "House for a Young Couple,"[7] 1904. Here each room is polarized around its own decorative theme, organized in patterns generating even a third dimension, with a richness of variety that the contemporary viewer can perceive as a delirious geometry. Describing the bedroom and the dressing room, Bertha Zuckerkandl wrote that the artist had introduced a distinctive note that had not yet been included in Modern interior decoration, that is, "the discreet Frou-Frou of the elegant lady."[8] Here the *Innendekoration* (interior decoration) functions as the allusive metaphor for the person who lives and acts in that interior.

Moser's lively interest in stage sets and temporary architecture (for example, the mounting of the exhibitions of the Secession, the Werkstätte, and the Kunstgewerbeschule) encouraged the use of such an evocative thrust underlying a sense of decoration as *explicative articulation* of the structure[9] as well as an abbreviation or mere metaphor of its function. In fact, according to Moser, stage sets in the theater should not reproduce the ambience realistically, but should evoke the text and adhere to the given space.[10] The interiors he designed predestine and catalyze situations; they seem to embody the possible theatricalization of the interior. This is nothing else, perhaps, than the revolutionary strategy of an interior designer endowed with a special pictorial, and not only architectonic, sensitivity.

This practice of designing virtual and not real space was accompanied by a growing intolerance of the clients' demands[11] and their rather dated laments

[4] G. Fanelli, "L'infinito ornamento," in *FMR*, November 1982, pp. 29-68.
[5] H. van de Velde, *Geschichte meines Leben*, Munich, 1962.
[6] H. Muthesius, *Das englische Haus*, Berlin, 1904. (English translation, *The English House*, London, 1980, p. 51).
[7] The photographs of all the interiors in this not-fully-identified house accompany a long article on Moser and the same house. See B. Zuckerkandl, "Koloman Moser," in *Dekorative Kunst*, vo. XII, 1904, pp. 329-344.
[8] Ibid, p. 336.
[9] The definition is Gombrich's, p. 267.
[10] Moser, p. 12.
[11] Ibid.

Armoire for the bedroom of the "House for a Young Couple," interior possibly realized in Berlin in 1903-04. (From *Dekorative Kunst*, 1904)

[12] G.C. Argan, "Ultimi veleni da Vienna," in *L'Espresso*, 14 August 1983, p. 64.

[13] Ibid.

[14] W.J. Schweiger, *Wiener Werkstätte: Kunst und Handwerk 1903-1932*, Vienna, 1982.

[15] H. Bahr, *Der englischer Styl* (1899), cited in Schweiger, *Wiener Werkstätte*, p. 14.

[16] Schweiger, *Wiener Werkstätte*, pp. 20-21.

[17] Ibid.

over the loss of the serenity in art, about which Moser's restless swings between pragmatism and a bad conscience are a vivid commentary. As Argan wrote of Klimt, he "did not heed this tension... through the old poetry-sick middle class and the new cupidity for monstrous profits."[12] It was not by chance, then, that he attempted to theatricalize that which had steered the bourgeois interior toward the non-representational. "As a culture is born," to quote Argan's penetrating article again, "one can see how the previous one dies,"[13] and Moser, like others, experimented with that dusk and dawn; in a certain sense, as a primary figure he held a privileged position from which to interpret that transition.

Hoffmann, Moser, and the Wiener Werkstätte

On 25 November 1899, a few days before the new century, the critic Hermann Bahr, mentor of Vienna's avant-garde and experimental artists, foresaw the birth in Austria of an artistic craftsmanship, which according to William Morris's precepts was to become the privileged place of dialectic integration between architect and executor, between projected and realized plan.[14] This integration could only take place if the designer were familiar with each detail of the artisan's process and if the artisan in turn were to appropriate the project, and its exact communicative value, as a whole. "Today we have an abundance of artists, and we also have artisans; what is missing is only... an organization comprehensive enough to be able to link art and artisan... with a gigantic atelier, a colony of laborers where the artists work with the artisans."[15] Bahr asked himself, finally, if to favor the reciprocal growth of art and craftsmanship, it would be opportune for artists who had already been collaborating together—such as Olbrich, Hoffmann, Böhm, Engelhart, and Moser—to unite to establish these communal works.

This enterprise was realized sooner than expected. As a matter of fact, in 1901 a sort of cooperative was founded by the neo-diplomats of the Kunstgewerbeschule, mostly pupils of Hoffmann and Moser. It was called Wiener Kunst im Hause and counted among its first associates Gisela Falke, Franz Messner, Jutta Sika, Wilhelm Schmidt, and Hans Vollmer.[16] Thanks also to the "spiritual patronage" of Hoffmann and Moser, the group did not lack projects; and the principal focus of their activity was group projects. So their interiors, as presented in the Christmas show of the Wiener Kunstgewerbeverein,[17] were works of *total* art in which each detail was worked out with great refinement, but which were to be considered collective works of art.

The Wiener Kunst im Hause realized Bahr's proposition only in part. The association did not have its own workshops and craftsmen, but had to have its projects realized by other companies or factories. As Hoffmann would record much later in his autobiography, the creation of workshops became an undeniable

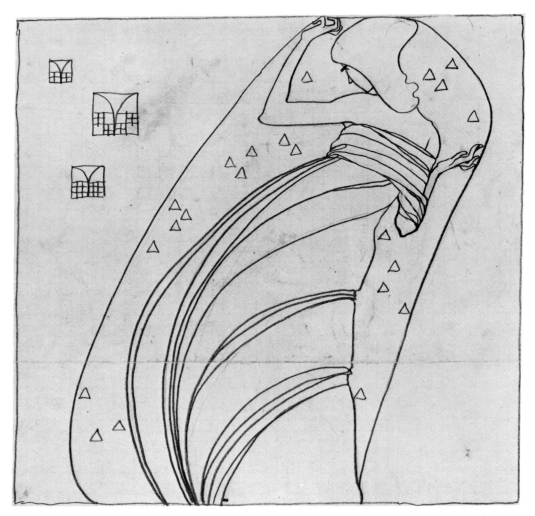

Design for tiles in embossed metal, 1904. (Collection J. Hummel, Vienna)

necessity; in fact, those Viennese mentioned were not equipped—and not only on the level of sheer volume capacity—to undertake "modern" projects. "The attempt to have our ideas realized by the existing companies failed due to the impossibility of counting on careful handwork."[18]

It was because of this that in November of 1902 Hoffmann and Moser, with the help of a silversmith and two blacksmiths, converted their Heumühlgasse no. 6 in District IV, into workshops for silver and metals. The next year this initiative was formalized in the Wiener Werkstätte in which, as it is known, two of the founders—Hoffmann and Moser—assumed the artistic directorship, and a third—Wärndorfer—the commercial administrative duties. The new headquarters were situated at Neustiftgasse 32/34, in District IV.

Much has been written, especially recently,[19] about the structural and cultural aims of the Wiener Werkstätte; not that the primary importance of this enterprise didn't lie in Hoffmann's and Moser's development of an original language, but rather in the spread of the Wienerstil throughout the world. It

[18] J. Hoffmann, "Selbstbiographie," 1950, published in *Ver Sacrum—Neue Folge*, 1972, p. 110.
[19] See among others, *Wien um 1900*, exhibition catalog, Vienna, 1964; *Die Wiener Werkstätte—Modernes Kunsthandwerk von 1903-1932*, exhibition catalog, Österreichisches Museum für angewandte Kunst, Vienna, 1967; N. Powell, *The Sacred Spring—The Arts in Vienna 1898-1918*, London, 1974; W. Fenz, *Kolo Moser*, Salzburg, 1976; *Vienna Moderne: 1898-1918*, catalog, Houston/New York, 1978-79; *Vienna—Turn of the Century—Art and Design*, exhibition catalog, London, 1979-80; D. Baroni and A. D'Auria, *Josef Hoffmann e la Wiener Werkstätte*, Milan, 1981; G. Fanelli and E. Godoli, *La Vienna di*

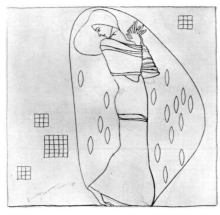

Design for tiles in embossed metal, 1904. (Private Collection, Vienna)

Hoffmann architetto della qualità, Rome/Bari, 1981; Schweiger, *Wiener Werkstätte*; D. Baroni and A. D'Auria, "Josef Hoffmann and the Wiener Werkstätte," in *Japan Interior Design*, n. 286, 1983, pp. 15-80; E.F. Sekler, *Josef Hoffmann*, Salzburg, 1982; W. Fenz, *Kolo Moser*, Salzburg/Vienna, 1984.

[20] See E.F. Sekler, "Mackintosh and Vienna," in *Architectural Review*, December 1968, now in N. Pevsner and J.M. Richards, *The Anti-Rationalist*, London, 1973, p. 85; and H.-H. Kossatz, "The Vienna Secession and Its Early Relations with Great Britain," in *Studio International*, n. 17/6, January 1971, p. 12.

[21] Moser records it himself in *Mein Werdegang*, p. 11.

[22] E.F. Sekler, "Mackintosh and Vienna," p. 140.

would be superfluous here, therefore, to go into such an elementary discourse. We will merely record the consistency and the magnitude of the initiative undertaken—it would suffice to record the culminating event at the Palais Stoclet—of the shows (Berlin, London, Vienna), of creations in all sectors of design, from jewelry to fashion, bookbinding to glass, furniture to architecture. It is necessary, however, to underline the derivative connection between the Werkstätte and the analogous preceding European initiatives upon which it was admittedly modeled, whether ideologically or organizationally.

Hoffmann and Moser looked first of all to those groups that had succeeded, in the last years of the nineteenth century or the first years of the twentieth, in joining theory to practice, in closing the gap between planning and realization, and in establishing the most dialectically possible rapport with the public—permitting it to act not as a client only, but as an active interlocutor. Nearby Germany offered more than one example, from the Vereinigten Werkstätte für Kunst im Handwerk, founded in Monaco in 1897 by Obrist, Pankok, Riemerschmid, Paul, Behrens, and others, to the Dresdener Werkstätte für Handwerkskunst, founded the following year by Karl Schmidt. But the one man that convinced Hoffmann and Moser of the validity of the *Werkstätte Prinzip* (the workshop principle) was in all probability the Englishman Ashbee, already well known to Hoffmann[20] and present in Vienna on the occasion of the eighth show of the Secession. In 1888 Ashbee had founded the Guild & School of Handicrafts, within a tradition based on theory as well as production. In Great Britain this had illustrious precedents, from Mackmurdo's Century Guild of 1882 to Crane and Day's Art Workers Guild of 1884; from the Home Art & Industrie Association of 1885 to the Arts & Crafts Exhibition Society inspired by Morris and founded by Crane in 1888.

Moreover, Hoffmann and Moser were encouraged and counseled by Meier-Graefe, the critic, merchant, and art collector, whom both had met in Paris at the World's Fair in 1900.[21] Mackintosh, also enthusiastic over the idea, was prodigal with suggestions and encouragement.[22] In Vienna at the eighth exposition of the Secession, their work was exhibited, evidently not by chance, alongside the works of Austrian designers and the best objects of the Maison Moderne of Meier-Graefe, of Ashbee's guild, of the Scottish group Mackintosh-McDonald-McNair, and of van de Velde. The latter, from 1899, was director of the workshops annexed to the Hohenzollern Kunstgwerbehaus in Berlin, an organization engaged in the promotion of the artistic craftsmanship.

The wish to compete with the best foreign products, and to draw a profit through the direct observation of the results attained outside Austria, motivated the organizers to select artists of that sort for the Viennese exhibition. Therefore we can assume that those invited constituted, for Moser and Hoffmann, a precise reference not only to their operational strategy but, really, to an expressive poetry and a focus on their formal repertory. Moser's and therefore Hoffmann's stylistic improvement, and their future association with the Werkstätte, owe much to the example of Ashbee, whose furniture, as I have observed, seemed to come from a "square planet... straightedged, rectangles, at ninety degrees... a kind of English Biedermeier, simple, solid, massive."[23] In that same period the Austrian scholar Bertha Zuckerkandl recognized in Ashbee "a versatile artist" who had produced in his London workshops objects which were considered "among the most precious models for Modern art."[24]

The intense admiration felt for Mackintosh and his group by the young Viennese is clearly a result of the substantial homogeneity displayed in the work of the Scotsmen and, a year later, in that of Hoffmann and Moser.[25] In 1904 an acute, although (as is well known) not objective, observer Hermann Muthesius related that in Mackintosh's group as in that of the young Viennese there was a definite rejection of the "floral" excesses of so much French and Belgian Art Nouveau. "On the Continent the Scottish encountered the most vivid approval, but without first participating at a show, these, particularly in Vienna, stimulated and catalyzed the changes in the world of forms so fruitfully, establishing for themselves and their leaders a permanent legacy."[26] Hoffmann's and Moser's first efforts in the field of *Innendekoration* (especially in the preparation of model interiors meant to be shown in exhibits of the Secession or the Wiener Werkstätte) show a marked tendency toward simplicity in the concept of furniture and in the sparseness of the environment—typical attitudes of Mackintosh's group. As Muthesius would observe again, for the Scottish designers the fundamental aim is the interior as artifice, "organic unity of color, style and feeling," so that the result is a "model of function and of spatial organization."[27] Finally, how could we not remark a close kinship between Mackintosh's room at the Secessionist exhibit—"a white room," as Hevesi wrote, "in what we call Brettlstil,"[28]—and the furniture that Hoffmann designed, reproductions of which accompanied his article *Einfache Möbel* (Simple Furniture)[29] or the connection between the use that Mackintosh and MacDonald made of the stylized female figure, and the abstract anthropomorphic ornaments—with obvious feminine connotations—so frequently used by Moser in his furniture?

It should be added, nevertheless, that the admiration of Moser and his young enthusiastic colleagues for Mackintosh's black and white, his decorative abstraction, his essential Secessionist linearity, or his high regard for the Spartan simplicity of Ashbee's objects, his old-manner-style functionalism, the solidity and the valuable design concessions of his furniture to craftsmanship—that admiration was not enough to justify the enthusiasm for models from such a distant world and style of life. On the contrary, the English model is rooted in a precise historical phase of Austrian culture, if only as an antidote to more invasive neighboring models. Among the "Anglophiles," we cite above all the example of Wagner, who advised his students to extend the "grand tour" to include England; of Loos, who never lost an opportunity to express his positive appreciation for English furniture and clothing; the Österreichisches Museum für Kunst und Industrie, which was built on the model of the Victoria and Albert in London and which regularly showed English objects and furniture

Cover for an album of designs for "simple furniture," probably for the Purkersdorf Sanatorium, 1903-04. (Hochschule für angewandte Kunst, Vienna)

[23] L. Hevesi, *Acht Jahre Sezession*, Vienna, 1906, p. 289.
[24] Schweiger, *Wiener Werkstätte*, p. 17.
[25] The works of the Mackintosh group had already been published in 1897; see G. White, "Some Glasgow Designers," in *The Studio*, XI, 1897, pp. 88-95; R. Billcliffe and P. Vergo, "Charles Rennie Mackintosh and the Austrian Art Revival," in *The Burlington Magazine*, n. 896, vol. CXIX, 1977, pp. 739-744.
[26] Muthesius.
[27] Ibid.
[28] Cited by Kossatz, p. 16.
[29] J. Hoffmann, "Einfache Möbel," in *Das Interieur*, II, 1901, pp. 193-208.

as models for the Viennese craftsmen;[30] and the Kunstgewerbeschule, where among the textbooks he used, Moser included Owen Jones's *The Grammar of Ornament.*

Another aspect of the Wiener Werkstätte that seems relevant is the importance Moser placed on directing the stylistic orientation of the cooperative toward a geometric-linear "style." That is, it is necessary in the first place to rescue Moser from the supremacy usually attributed to Hoffmann within their partnership. It involves, in short, isolating Moser's function within the context of the Wiener Werkstätte and, to some extent, within the Secession.

While recognizing that Hoffmann and Moser played different, although certainly complementary, and at times alternate, roles in the Werkstätte, it is necessary to confirm that their creative association left a unified cultural and artistic legacy. Joseph August Lux significantly entitles an article on the Wiener Werkstätte, "Hoffmann-Moser;"[31] and about sixty years later, at the awakening of a critical and historical interest in the Werkstätte that even now shows no sign of lessening, Wilhelm Mrazek named the period from the foundation in 1903 to the First World War (1915) as the "Hoffmann-Moser period". This is to reaffirm the importance of the Moser contribution, even after 1907, the year he left the company.

In fact, the extension of the "Moser" period seems to us excessive, particularly if one considers the stylistic evolution of Moser following the Czeschka influence, with the introduction of elliptic and spiral motifs, from 1906 on. Not to mention the contributions of Wimmer and then Peche—in 1908 and 1915—who, with their designs filled with effeminate grace and Rococo echoes, radically changed the formal direction of the Werkstätte.[32] At any rate, at least up to 1908-10, "geometric-linear" products continued to be produced, while Moser, even from a distance, perhaps through his graphic designs, continued to be an interlocutor and a model for Hoffmann and other ex-associates.

The rapport of friendship-collaboration between Moser and Hoffmann stemmed from their contact in 1895 at the activist community in the Siebner Club, in the Künstlerhaus in 1896, and in the Secession the following year. Immersed in the very ambience of the Secession, the two realized their first works together: for example, pages in *Ver Sacrum*, in which one would design the frame and the other the headings; the installations of the Austrian pavilion at the World's Fair in Paris, 1900; or the organization of some of the Secession's periodic shows. Together they designed magazine covers for the *Deutsche Österreichische Literaturgeschichte*. In 1898 Hoffmann designed the furniture for a friend's studio; there is the famous photograph taken of him sitting in his *Karrenförmigen Stühle* (carriage-wheel chairs) that furnished the studio. In 1899 Hoffmann used Moser's fabric, *Forellenreigen* (with a trout motif) for some living room furniture. In the same year, Moser executed a stained-glass window for a candle shop, Hoffmann's "Apollo." Between 1899 and 1900 Moser's tapestries were used in two Hoffmann interiors: one with a leaf motif for Villa Pollak, and the other, *Föhn*, executed by Backhausen in the Ministry office of the same

[30] A. D'Auria, *Il fantasma del nuovo*, in D. Baroni and A. D'Auria, 1981, pp. 27-34.
[31] J.A. Lux, "Josef Hoffmann—Koloman Moser (Wiener Werkstätte)," in *Deutsche Kunst und Dekoration*, n. 15, 1904-05, pp. 7-14.
[32] W. Mrazek, "Die Wiener Werkstätte," in *Die Wiener Werkstätte—Modernes Kunsthandwerk von 1903-1932*, p. 16.

client. In 1902 Hoffmann placed one of his colleague's windows in the installation of the Viennese Secession's room at the Kunstausstellung in Düsseldorf.

At the founding of the Wiener Werkstätte the two prepared the showrooms together; the workshop sections included jewelry, metal, cabinetry, and leather. The work spaces were exemplary—modern and bright, equipped with all the toilet facilities. The various sections were distinguished by different colors: an ideal setting for creative work. The display rooms were spacious and bright; the furniture and objects were arranged in configurations suggestive of how the various pieces might be arrayed and how they might modify the home, once brought home by the buyer.

In the Werkstätte, Hoffmann's and Moser's joint work naturally was intensified; neither one renounced his own authority, distinguishing individual works and projects with a stamp or monogram. Nevertheless, in consulting the thousands of photographic images in the society's archives,[33] it may be seen that many objects—especially works in metal or leather or even furniture—and many interiors do not bear any label, whereas others—and these comprise less than half—are diligently attributed to one or the other. Nevertheless, these are undoubtedly the objects and interiors of Hoffmann and/or Moser, and we can reasonably suppose that—wherever it is not a matter of variations on an idea executed by the *Meister* (Masters) of the workshops—these are the products of a joint effort. This difficulty in attributing a project to one or the other says much about the perfect equality of the two designers within the Werkstätte. It was not infrequent that in the rediscovery of an original design the attribution of some furniture or an interior would be changed from one to the other, as was recently the case with some lacquered furniture in the *Toilettenzimmer* (dressing room) or some chairs at the Wittgenstein House, first unsuspectingly attributed to Hoffmann, and only recently, after the rediscovery of the original drawings, assigned to Moser.[34]

"If you really want to know if one thing is Hoffmann's or Moser's, all you need to do is find out who was attracted to it. The women are fascinated by Moser, the men run to Hoffmann." Klimt's amused observation seems to correlate with Hevesi's concise appraisal when he speaks of Hoffmann's work having "elegant logic," and Moser's, "refined poetry."[35] Wilhelm Fred, commenting on the furniture shown at the eighth Secessionist exhibit, declared that Moser was absolutely "the more gifted one."[36]

But what best helps us to determine the value of each man's contribution within the Moser-Hoffmann collaboration is possibly Hoffmann's own opinion: "It was stupefying how Moser, even as a painter, was able to penetrate the secrets of constructive techniques, and how quickly he was able to discern the inexactitude and defects generated by a common error."[37] Amelia Levetus, a Viennese correspondent for *The Studio*, wrote the following in an article on the development of design in Austria: "Professor Moser is an extraordinary man. It is difficult to find a sector in the applied arts in which he hasn't put himself to the test... Hoffmann and Moser have created a new style in the decorative

[33] See *Archiv der Wiener Werkstätte*, Österreichisches Museum für angewandte Kunst, Vienna.

[34] For the *Toilettenzimmer*, see exhibition catalog *Vienna Moderne: 1898-1918*, pp. 96-97, and Baroni and D'Auria, 1981. For some chairs for the Hermann Wittgenstein house, see *Archiv der Wiener Werkstätte*, vol. XIII; the armchair is attributed to Hoffmann in V.J. Behal, *Möbel des Jugendstil* (Sammlung der Österreichisches Museum für angewandte Kunst), Vienna, 1981, pp. 158-59; the archive of the Hochschule für angewandte Kunst in Vienna includes a drawing in Moser's collection signed "K.M.," with scale drawings of the armchair and of a divan. Other than these mistaken attributions, we can witness the difficulties in assigning double attributions, either in cases when, from time to time, certain projects were considered by one or the other (as I have already shown: see D'Auria, p. 64), or in the case when there is one (or more) version of a drawing and the signatures contradict each other (as, for example, the maquette for the Cabaret Fledermaus, of which there is a version signed by Moser, see Fenz, 1984, photograph on p. 214, and one signed Lö[ffler], see *Bertold Löffler (1874-1960)*, edited by H. Adamek, exhibition catalog, the Austrian Institute, New York, 1982, Vienna, 1981, p. 21).

[35] L. Hevesi, *Altkunst-Neukunst: Wien 1894-1908*, Vienna, 1919, p. 227.

[36] W. Fred, "Die Wiener Sezession: VIII Ausstellung," in *Innen-Dekoration*, n. 12, 1901, p. 32.

[37] Hoffmann, p. 112.

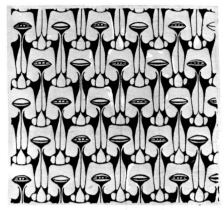

Pattern study, 1899. (Hochschule für angewandte Kunst, Vienna)

Study for marquetry for *Cigar Cabinet*, 1900. (Private Collection, Vienna)

and applied arts, an essentially Viennese style: and even if they have derived much from other schools, their own school bears an unmistakable signature thanks to which it will always be possible to recognize it in the future as the Hoffmann and Moser school."[38] Again, according to Hoffmann: "Moser's predisposition toward two-dimensional art and for every kind of invention in the applied arts turned out to be fabulous. After all, he stimulated and promoted new initiatives."[39]

Moser was the "stimulator," then, who continually invented new stylistic solutions and investigated new formal theories, leaving the experimentation to others and the development to Hoffmann, "the assimilator," of course, who "allowed himself to be influenced to a great degree in order to develop the stimulus respecting its own characteristic style."[40]

In light of this emerging picture, Moser's participation in works to which Hoffmann was the main contributor was more than marginal, although somewhat limited. We refer especially to the Purkersdorf Sanatorium where, whether in terms of the general project (the treatment of the facades, for example) or in the interior design, there is no mistaking Moser's contribution. It would suffice to look at the first houses built by Hoffmann between 1900 and 1903 on the Hohe Warte and to compare their lively and exuberant architecture, admittedly inspired by Anglo-Saxon models, with the refined decorum of the sanatorium. Here there is concrete testimony of Moser's collaboration in the interior design of the rooms for men and women; and, as remarked above, we may also attribute to Moser the armchairs Hoffmann used in the Halle. The same year, 1904, the two of them were commissioned with the dining room furniture for Editha Mutner-Markhof, Moser's future mother-in-law. In the Lederer and Hermann Wittgenstein houses around 1904, Moser was involved in particular with the windows and other so-called accessory elements. In the Remy House, of the same period, assorted pieces of Moser's and Hoffmann's furniture were used in the interior decor.[41]

In other works, especially those for friends or associates of the Werkstätte or show displays, the collaboration between the two became closer, and in trying to distinguish each one's responsibility in the project, one ends up attributing the projects equally to both. This was the case with the fashion atelier of the Flöge sisters in 1904, and of the Wärndorfer House of the same period; of the exhibition in Berlin, the Wiener Werkstätte's first in 1904, or the one in London in the Imperial Royal Austria Exhibition in 1906, and the show at the Galerie Miethke in Vienna in 1905.

The big exhibition in Berlin, held in the Hohenzollern Kunstgewerbehaus, lasted four months and was very successful. In direct consequence the Werkstätte got some important commissions for the interior design of the Berlin house of Margarethe Stonborough, Karl Wittgenstein's daughter; and the first official printing job from the government: the centennial volume of the State printers. From that year on, moreover, all the principal magazines throughout Europe rushed with interest to the work of the Werkstätte—from *The Studio*

[38] A.S. Levetus, "Modern Decorative Art in Austria," in *The Art Revival in Austria*, edited by Ch. Holme, in *The Studio*, a special issue, 1906.
[39] J. Hoffmann, "Meine Arbeit," lecture, in Schweiger, *Wiener Werkstätte*, p. 32.
[40] Ibid.
[41] Sekler, *Josef Hoffmann*, p. 291.

to *Zeitschrift für Innendekoration*, to *Dekorative Kunst*, which published two long articles by Bertha Zuckerkandl on Hoffmann and Moser,[42] to *Deutsche Kunst und Dekoration*, which between 1904 and 1911 published twelve special numbers dedicated to the Wiener Werkstätte. There was no lack of enthusiastic comments: Hevesi spoke of the "felicitous initiative of applied idealism," of "an artistic artisan" devoid of affectation, of a style which, although it "had a certain coldness," was "refreshing" after the orgy of color of the preceding years.[43] Delighted, Meier-Graefe declared with satisfaction, "Now that artists have become workers, art has arrived."[44]

This success with the public met all expectation. The Werkstätte planned every detail of their public image: for example, the invoices, stationery, wrapping paper, and even the typeface of the typewriter were designed and copyrighted with public relations in mind.

Moser drew up the monogram with the double *W*, which upside down was a double *M* already used in the lettering for the cover of *Bummerlei* in 1896.[45] The rose trademark may be attributed to Hoffmann, given the similarity to an abstract decoration executed by him around 1901 in a decorative mural.[46] The prestige of that double *W* and that rose spread throughout the continent in a few years. When Moser, for reasons we shall soon learn, left the Wiener Werkstätte in 1907, the world of applied arts was at a historical turning point. The Deutsche Werkbund foundation decreed the definitive burial of Morrisian romanticism and its dream of a panartistic artisanship. Muthesius's and Rathenau's initiatives ran on the same side of history, while the Werkstätte, ideology aside, was seen, especially with an increasingly Baroque accent and Biedermeier style owed to Wimmer and Löffler, as a surviving company of the decadent, decorative, and eclectic nineteenth century. Under the steady strain of an anxiety that took on ever new forms, almost a projection of those collaborative ventures, the truest image of those last but fervid years of their empire, the associates of the Werkstätte, the Secessionists, and the Secessionists of the Secession were starting to imitate themselves.

In the perspective of this singular and by now emblematic decline, Moser's career appears endowed with its own clear specificity, fraught as it was with tensions and not immediately identifiable causes, somewhat different from those of the group of "obsoletes" of which he formed part.

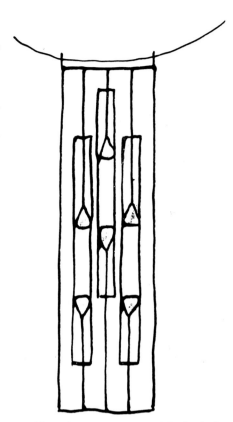

Necklace design, ca. 1903. (Hochschule für angewandte Kunst, Vienna)

From Design for the Elite to Industrial Projects

"For the Viennese, Moser was the man of squares; many thought he had invented the checkerboard... He let them believe it... Little by little he retired into silence leaving behind even his last few friends. He hid himself so well that perhaps it would take first years to find out what really happened."[47] With these words Hermann Bahr mourned the premature death, in 1918, of his friend Moser, and also the disconcerting fact that the artist had left behind

42 B. Zuckerkandl, "Josef Hoffmann," in *Dekorative Kunst*, vol. VII, 1903-04, pp. 1-15, and "Koloman Moser," in *Dekorative Kunst*.
43 Hevesi, *Acht Jahre Sezession*, pp. 483-486.
44 Schweiger, *Wiener Werkstätte*, p. 20.
45 E. Pötzl, *Bummelei*, Vienna, 1896; Schweiger, *Wiener Werkstätte*, pp. 170-71.
46 It is about the H. Koller House of 1901-02. See Sekler, *Josef Hoffmann*, p. 270.
47 Bahr, pp. 161-63.

Advertisement for J.&J. Kohn, ca. 1902.

Book cover for *Österreichische Kunst des XIX Jarhhunderts* by Ludwig Hevesi, Vienna, 1904.

48 B. Zuckerkandl, "Kolo Moser— Galerie Miethke," in *Wiener Allgemeine Zeitung*, 13 March 1911, cited in Schweiger, *Wiener Werkstätte*, p. 32.
49 Moser, p. 9.
50 F. Servaes, *Grüsse am Wien*, Berlin/Vienna/Leipzig, 1948, cited in Schweiger, *Kolo Moser—Ein biographische Skizze*, in *Kolo Moser*, p. 15.
51 Cited by Schweiger, *Kolo Moser*, p. 19.
52 Schweiger, *Wiener Werkstätte*, p. 192.

such weak traces. Would Moser's few, if highly qualified, contributions to all the sectors of applied art have been enough to guarantee the place he was due in the history of design? Even though through his mastery he had spurred experimentation and new orientations in a whole generation of artists, for a long time Moser had not been at the center of critical attention as might have been expected.

Probably one of the causes of this underestimation can be found in Moser's own personality, which was elusive and devoid of any outstanding characteristics—save the inverted and negative one of having none. It was not by chance, for example, that Moser had individualized and initiated many experimental routes without pursuing any in depth, without showing the determination of one who exists and acts with an eye on history. Not at all a man of "practical and organizational capacity," as Bertha Zuckerkandl points out, Moser "as soon as he strikes a spark is no longer interested."[48]

Moser's extraordinary versatility in every aspect of design could hence be easily attributed to innate talent. Hoffmann himself was fascinated by him: recalling his past intense experiences with his friend and colleague, he spoke of Moser with a profound nostalgia, underlining his fervor and inexhaustible inventiveness conjoined with a perfect knowledge and mastery of the artisanal procedures. Moser, with the calm modesty that always distinguished him, in an autobiographical note attributed his abilities to his childhood experiences in the Theresianum, a school where his father was employed as treasurer and where the young Moser had daily contact with the craftsmen of the complex. "Later, many would marvel at my technical versatility in many trades, and at my extensive knowledge of carpentry, bookbinding, and metalworking... Everybody knows that a child gets into everything. When he sees something, he learns it immediately. In just this way I learned from the most diverse masters: I bound books, built rabbit hutches, sewed clothes, learned how to cut wood on a lathe and, from the gardener, I learned how to create the most wonderful flower arrangements. Then it was an entertaining and charming game which later became a decisively important element and which made me to feel at home in the field of applied arts."[49]

Franz Servaes coined the phrase "decorative Kleinkunstgenie"[50] for Moser, and Bahr the epithet "Tausendkünstler" (which more or less means expert in a thousand arts).[51] Their opinions were based on Moser's first and immediately remarkable tests as a designer at the exhibition organized by the Secession, or at the Kunstgewerbeschule where he taught "decoration": for example, a set of twelve glasses shown at the World's Fair in Paris, 1900, a success at an auction competition won by Moser in the first year of the Kunstgewerbemuseum;[52] or the furniture and windows shown at the Secession's eighth exhibit, among which was the dresser *Der reiche Fischzug* (The Rich Catch of Fish), which was acquired by the Minister of Culture, Ritter von Hartel.

Under the double standard of "the total work of art" and "art everywhere," Hoffmann and Moser designed everything, always attentive to the joint requirements of their continuous evolution and development. The contribution of the objects and furniture of the two Austrian designers towards the development and success of functionalist requests and the enrichment of a formal repertory, which, with a few further simplifications, became the legacy of rationalism, is perhaps, paradoxically, an even more important result of the theories and didactics of an architect considered one of the fathers of the Modern movement, Otto Wagner. Hoffmann and Moser elaborated their theories and programs and taught more than one generation of students at the Kunstgewerbeschule, some of whom turned out to be outstandingly gifted. But this was without a doubt the result of their having had the finest teachers.

In 1901, both Moser and Hoffmann, a big step forward was carried out that freed them definitively from the provincialism that for at least thirty years had suffocated Austrian art, allowing them to set forth on the road already undertaken by their British colleagues, from Baillie Scott to Mackintosh, Voysey, and Ashbee. Hoffmann published *Einfache Möbel*, an essay dedicated to the need for "simple furniture," and annotated by numerous drawings and vignettes depicting furniture and interiors.[53] Moser published *Flächenschmuck*, an album of thirty plates with pattern designs on the recto and verso of each page, for wallpaper, fabrics and carpets.[54] These two publications, perfectly balanced poetic manifestations, mirrored each other: Hoffmann proposed an interaction with the structure and a modification of space, intended as a kind of total artifact through a dialectic between the surroundings, the plastic presence of the furniture and objects; Moser instead tended toward a more virtual rather than a physical sense of space, a more perceptual rather than tactile approach, in the direction of pure vision.

At any rate Moser appropriated the functionalist aesthetic prefigured in *Einfache Möbel* and, with a greater vehemence than Hoffmann, freed himself from Olbrich's sinuosities. A first, partial proof of this was the invention—or we should say rediscovery—of the square motif. This motif, which came to characterize the first phase of the Wiener Werkstätte, was certainly partially taken from Mackintosh and Olbrich,[55] used as a graphic frame in an issue of *Ver Sacrum* of 1901,[56] and from then on was adopted as a stylistic convention—perhaps in a somewhat glib and brusque way—in all of Moser's and Hoffmann's productions and marked the first phase of the Wiener Werkstätte.

The families of forms found in Moser's work as a designer, one should note, had already been tested in print, published by *Ver Sacrum* or *Die Fläche*, or on numerous friezes or publications designed by Moser for other publications.

In this sense the activity of the graphic artist and that of the designer were closely complementary; the first took place in the workshop in a spirit of free play and experimentation; the second, more immediately involved with production, took place through concrete application. Examples of this are Backhausen's fabric designs of 1900, published in *Ver Sacrum*; and the square carpet with the squares and diamonds in white, black and red, realized by Backhausen around 1903, placed by Moser in the boudoir of "Frau Dr. M."[57]

Clock design, ca. 1901. (Private Collection, Vienna)

[53] Ibid.
[54] K. Moser, "Flächenschmuck," in the series *Die Quelle*, Vienna/Leipzig, 1901.
[55] For Mackintosh, the checkerboard or treillis motifs recalled the vernacular of Scottish tradition. Muthesius would count these motifs among those which give a "patriarchal air" to modern Scottish residences (see *Das englische Haus*, p. 180). Olbrich, in his ornamental exuberance, included a checkerboard decoration in many projects, from the Römheld House of 1900, where they are seen scattered on the surface of the dining room and living room.
[56] See "Arno-Holz-Heft," in *Ver Sacrum*, IV, 1901.
[57] Published in *Das Interieur*, IV, 1903, p. 48.

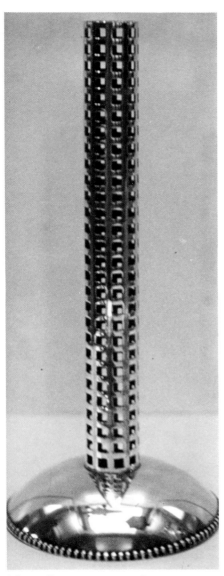

Silver flower vase, made at Wiener Werkstätte, 1905.

[58] See "Drei Spiele von Rainer Maria Rilke," in *Ver Sacrum*, IV, 1901.
[59] See the plans for a *Blumenvase* in the Moser Estate of the Österreichisches Museum für angewandte Kunst in Vienna, vol. XXII, and the volume *Zur Feier des Einhundertjahrigen Bestandes der K.K. Hof-und Staatsdruckerei*, Vienna, November 1904.
[60] B. Zuckerkandl, "Erinnerungen an Kolo Moser," in *Neues Wiener Journal*, 23 January 1927, cited in Schweiger, *Kolo Moser*, p. 17.

and very similar to the graphics accompanying one of Rilke's contributions to *Ver Sacrum* in 1901;[58] or the enamel decorations of a prismatic flower vase executed by the Werkstätte and used as the frontispiece of the creative volume on the centennial of the State press in 1904.[59] It would be impossible to pinpoint the exact moment of exchange between graphic and typographic solutions and their repeated application in decorative modules used as structural elements in displays, in windows, objects, furniture: from the frieze of dancers for the Secession to "reciprocal" motifs of fish, birds, or flowers on furniture or fabrics, in the monochromatic filigree used for the displays at showplaces; or the stylized anthropomorphic figures that often counterpointed abstract decorations or unworked surfaces.

As a designer, Moser played two different roles: the one involving the craftsmen and the Wiener Werkstätte, and the other having to do with industry. We must not forget his role as consultant—a side role, but, as will be seen, not secondary to several publishing houses, from Bruckmann to Fischer, from Gerlach to Koch, from Fromme to Staatsdruckerei. The furniture made by Portois & Fix, the pianos built by Stingl, the necklaces designed by Scheid and Rozet & Fischmeister, the iridescent vases, products of Loetz Company, not to mention the jewelry, bookbindings, batik paper, silver, ceramics, and furniture executed by the Wiener Werkstätte are without a doubt elite products, destined for elegant use and selected as investments and for their cultural value. For example, women such as Emilie Flöge, Broncia Koller, and Alma Mahler had themselves photographed wearing, as a sign of distinction, some of Moser's jewelry.

The trellis motifs (Kistenstil) and the objects of lattice metal (*Gittenwerk*), so common in the work of the Werkstätte, made Moser certainly more famous than he, by temperament, would have wished. Zuckerkandl said that Moser "became popular in Vienna through his square-shaped objects. Naturally, popular in the sense of causing a great stir. It was an object of discussion whether Moser was crazy or a drunkard, if he wanted to make an impression... But the public and the critics understood next to nothing."[60] Certainly, as we have already seen, Moser's work was not always misunderstood, but we cannot dismiss the possibility that such negative opinions forced him to leave the Werkstätte in 1907 to dedicate himself almost exclusively to stage sets and painting.

In the Werkstätte, Moser dedicated much of his attention to papermaking and bookbinding. A bookbinding exhibit was given at the Galerie Miethke, of which Carl Moll was artistic director, in 1905. The following year Moser, Hoffmann, and Böhm participated in the International Buchbindekunstausstellung (International Exhibit of Artistic Bookbinding) in Frankfurt. Another field in which Moser distinguished himself was glass and silver tableware. In 1905 he participated with Hoffmann in the show "Der gedeckte Tisch" (The Well-Set Table) organized by the Museum of Applied Arts in Brno. Their participation was a success in that the museum made an acquisition (the first time that a State institution purchased objects from the Werkstätte), a set of silver

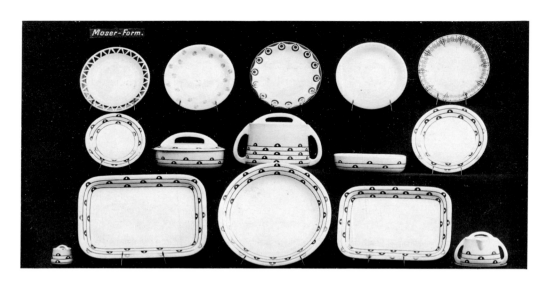

Porcelain by the "Moserschule" for Böck products, 1901-02.

flatware by Hoffmann and Moser.[61] The following year a show on the same theme was organized in the Wiener Werkstätte's new headquarters. For the occasion Moser designed innovative new shapes of bread and pasta, receiving, naturally, some unfavorable comments.[62]

It would be opportune at this point to turn to the second field in which Moser was active as a designer: that is, industry. The rapport between industry and design in Vienna at the beginning of the century was certainly not an easy one. "In principle," writes Moser, "we had to fight hard against the rigid conservatism of the large Viennese companies. We had to offer our drawings aggressively and literally impose them without asking for compensation, but only a percentage."[63] But Moser succeeded in establishing a close rapport with different industries, and this collaboration was the source of a reciprocal advantage: for the companies it was a matter of greatly raising the standard of quality, while the designer had the opportunity to leave more permanent traces of his work than would have been possible in his brief stay at the Werkstätte (given the attention generally paid to Moser by contemporary historians).

The first printing house that worked with Moser was Backhausen & Söhne, which, among other things, produced many fabrics on behalf of the Wiener Werkstätte. Backhausen produced Moser's upholstery material *Blumenerwachen* of 1899, *Gräser, Abimelech, Palmblatt, Florida, Hafis*, all from 1900-1902, and others, without a title to identify them in the absence of images. The same firm, again using a Moser design, produced a fabric for the Secession and Kunstgewerbeschule showrooms at the Paris Exhibition in 1900. As for Backhausen, he drew up the trademark and was in charge of graphics.

Relations with the Bakalowits glassware company began when they produced the set of twelve glasses with which Moser won the competition already mentioned, in 1899. In 1900 the collaboration was made formal, and from that date the firm radically changed its own production. With regard to this Hevesi commented, "With Koloman Moser Bakalowits has secured itself a creative

61 Schweiger, *Wiener Werkstätte*, p. 44.
62 Ibid, p. 60.
63 Moser, p. 4.

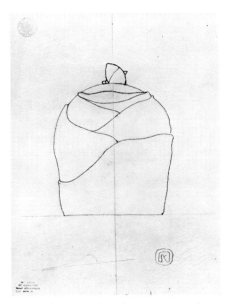

Design for sugar bowl in pinecone shape for Böck Ceramics, 1900. (Collection J. Hummel, Vienna)

talent which can stamp his originality in glass, in large as well as in small things."[64] Moser became a consultant to the Böck ceramic company in 1900, and other industries, such as the Austrian Loetz, around 1900; and the Rheinglashütte Ehrenfeld of Cologne, in 1903, made sets of glassware designed by him.

In interior decoration Moser collaborated ar first with Kohn, a business that produced bentwood furniture in the manner of Thonet. For this concern Moser was in charge of the trademark and public relations, and around 1901, he designed a set of furniture for a waiting room, which included a showcase, a divan, armchairs, and a table, in bent beechwood strips and plywood, with trimmings and fittings in brass. Similar to this furniture was a dressing table, presumably of the same year. Kohn's catalogue also included other pieces such as a magazine stand, armchairs, tables, perhaps attributable to Moser but, as was the custom of the time, presented without the designer's specifications. For Kohn, Moser in 1901 designed a set for a small living room, including a sofa, an armchair, and a chair. Around 1901 Thonet probably produced a hat stand. For Prag-Rudniker, a firm specializing in wicker furniture, in 1903 Moser designed a straw-bottomed chair with a back in interwoven strips in a checker design. This chair was produced in two versions, with and without arms, and clearly harked back to models of popular, and not only Austrian, traditions. In the preceding year Prag-Rudniker had produced a variant of the celebrated white lacquer cubic armchair with the vertical axes that Moser used in 1903 for the Klimt room at the Secession's eighteenth show, and which was placed soon after in the Halle of the Sanatorium Purkersdorf.

Finally, it is time to turn to areas in which Moser was seriously involved and of which little has been specifically said: that is, upholstery material (from 1905 on, Moser designed more than 300 fabrics for the Wiener Werkstätte) and women's fashions. Moser's involvement in women's fashions and particularly his active promotion of "Reformkleid" (reform dress), a movement for the reform of women's clothing, is proof of the pressure put on artists and designers at the turn of the century to become involved with each aspect of their projects and to influence every facet of the world of artifacts, while nevertheless keeping in mind an overall plan—even an ideology—dedicated to the renewal of the constructed world.

The first one to think of freeing women from the unhygienic constriction of the brassiere and the hypocrisy of padding was, not by chance, William Morris. The *Reformkleid* movement had as one of its principal theoreticians Paul Schultze-Naumburg,[65] leader of the Kulturarbeiten group, a kind of German Arts & Crafts, who was among the founders, in 1907, of the Deutscher Werkbund. In 1901 Schultze-Naumburg published a book on body care as a basis for the reform of clothing;[66] the thesis was that through the rediscovery of the female body, the *heilige Gefäss* (sacred vessel), one could restore the ethical and aesthetic value of the body-clothing system. In 1900, invited by the director of the Kaiser Wilhelm Museum of Krefeld, the most important artists work-

[64] Quoted by Schweiger, *Wiener Werkstätte*, pp. 192-94.
[65] O. Birkner, "Il nuovo stile di vita," in *Werkbund—Germania Austria Svizzera*, edited by L. Burkhardt, Venice, 1977, p. 52.
[66] P. Schultze-Naumburg, *Die Kultur des Weiblichen Körpers als Grundlage der Frauenkleidung*, Berlin, 1901.

ing in Germany at the time—from Pankok to van de Velde, from Riemerschmid to Schultze-Namburg—furnished sketches for a "Sonderausstellung moderner Damenkostüme."[67] The Dresdener Werkstätte organized a show around the same theme in Dresden in 1904.

In Vienna Loos had already been fighting since 1898 for a reform of men's as well as women's clothing.[68] Hoffmann also, in an article of 1898, had theorized on the reform of fashion.[69] The simplicity and severe functionalism of Loos's proposals however, were quite removed from those of the Viennese artists who, from Moser to Klimt, from Hoffmann to Wimmer,[70] ventured, from the first year of the century, to make dress designs.

By the end of 1906 it was Moser, who in 1900 had already designed an entire collection of reformed clothes,[71] who turned out to be the most incisive in following the direction theorized by Schultze-Naumburg. The novelty of his designs, which were simple and in some ways traditional, consisted in their simplicity of line, at times recalling a kimono, and in the absence of added elements such as lace, fringes, and crinolines. Moser's lesson was fruitfully taken up by his student Wimmer-Wisgrill, founder, among other things, of the department of fashion at the Wiener Werkstätte in 1910.[72]

At the end of this concise review of Moser's involvement with fashion design we can begin to realize what Hevesi meant when he said that during the first years of the new century one "Moser-ed" in every field.[73]

Another field in which Moser distinguished himself and left a permanent mark was, without a doubt, teaching. It should be noted that in German culture those who were considered the founders of the Modern movement were the architects, who at the beginning of the century were officially entrusted with the State's educational system; from Poelzig to Behrens, from van de Velde to Schumacher, from Riemerschmid to Wagner, from Hoffmann to Czeschka to Moser. In Vienna in particular, great importance was placed on Wagner's field, architecture, and on Hoffmann's and Moser's field, applied arts.

From 1898 until his death in 1918, Moser was on the teaching staff at the Kunstgewerbeschule, first as visiting teacher and after a year as a regular faculty member. Looking through the yearbooks of his students in the various classes on decoration, some significant names from Austrian design in the period between the two wars may be found. Among those who studied with Moser were Leopold Forstner, founder in 1906 of the Wiener Mosaik Werkstätte; Berthold Löffler, who with Powolny founded the Wiener Keramik in 1905; Jutta Sika, Therese Trethan, and Marietta Peyfuss who in 1901 began the Wiener Kunst im Hause; Ugo Zovetti who later became Moser's assistant; Eduard Wimmer who stepped into Moser's position in the Wiener Werkstätte when he left it in 1907; and Johanna Hollmann, Gustav Kalhammer, Anton Hofer, Oswald Haerdtl, and many others.

Sika, Trethan, and Forstner were among Moser's first students in 1899 and were among the founders of the Wiener Kunst im Hause; its supporters were, as we have seen, for the most part Hoffmann's and Moser's students. The group

[67] Birkner, p. 53, and "Sonderausstellung moderner Damenkostüme," in Dekorative Kunst, VI, 1900.
[68] See A. Loos, "La moda maschile," 1898, and "Moda femminile," 1898, collected in Ins Leere gesprochen, Paris, 1921. See also Das Andere, n. 1, 1903, p. 8.
[69] J. Hoffmann, "Das individuelle Kleid," in Die Wage, 4 April 1898, pp. 251-52; see Schweiger, Wiener Werkstätte, p. 223.
[70] Under "Secessionist" fashion one can find, among others, 200 Jahre Mode in Wien, exhibition catalog, Historisches Museum der Stadt Wien, Vienna, 1976.
[71] Schweiger, Kolo Moser, p. 19.
[72] Wimmer-Wisgrill—Modeentwürfe 1912-1927, exhibition catalog, Hochschule für angewandte Kunst, Vienna, 1983.
[73] Moser, p. 11.

Bedroom, executed by the Wiener Werkstätte. (From *The Studio Yearbook*, 1910)

participated in the Secession's fifteenth exhibit, which confirmed the success of Moser's school to the public at large. Most important in addition to the existence of the school itself, was the fresh energy that this school brought to the Wiener Werkstätte, which, it is well known, took into partnership many of Hoffmann's, Moser's, and Czeschka's freshly graduated students. The rapport between the Kunstgewerbeschule and the Werkstätte was an organic one, in which educational and professional activities were exchanged reciprocally; in particular, many of the artists of the cooperative became in turn teachers in the school of applied arts. As Alfred Roller—a teacher, like Moser, since 1899—wrote, "a generous blood has nourished teaching and living here."[74]

Moser's students contributed decisively to the abandonment of historical tendencies, and soon after, to the overthrow of the flora-decorativeness of the Jugendstil in many areas of the applied arts in which they were active, especially in the production of jewelry, glass, and ceramics.[75]

In 1900 Moser started to collaborate with some of his students at the glassware factory of Bakalowits and at Böck's porcelain factory. The plans were signed "Schule Prof. Kolo Moser," testimonial to the precise application of his precepts to the design project. This signature, which became a "mark of great quality,"[76] should not, however, lead us to believe that the various projects were stylistically uniform and overrun by the Master's models. On the contrary, Moser did not impose his own style on his students; but rather stimulated creativity through his support of individuality.

The Function of Form: Furniture and Fittings

In tune with the artistic avant-garde movements throughout Europe, the Secession demanded that equal importance be given to the *Kleinkunst* (the minor or applied arts) in relation to the noble arts of architecture, painting and sculpture. This cause could not have been better championed than by Hoffmann and Moser.

The Secession's importance, and that of its artists, within the context of art history can be attributed almost entirely to the importance acquired by design objects and interior decorating within the field of architecture during this time. According to the Anglo-Saxon historian, F. Witford, rather than presaging a new cultural season, the Secession marked the conclusion of an era, of a way of conceiving art and artists,[77] at least where the major arts—particularly painting and sculpture—were concerned. At the Secession, the applied arts were one of the most advanced aspects of the new art and of its insistence on a radical revision of the relationship between artists and society, which gave birth, as we all know, to the movement of Modern architecture. Moreover, it was in the fields of design and *Innenkunst* (interior decoration), rather than in architecture, that Austrian art made its mark within the context of Art Nouveau.

As a furniture designer, Moser, who until then had been a painter and graphic

[74] A. Roller, "L'école d'arts appliqués," in *L'Amour de l'Art*, IV, 1923, p. 653. Also A.S. Levetus, "The Craft Schools of Austria," in *The Studio*, n. 35, 1905, p. 206.
[75] Schweiger, *Wiener Werkstätte*, p. 191.
[76] Ibid, p. 200.
[77] F. Whitford, "Ends and Beginnings: Viennese Art at the Turn of the Century," in *Studio International*, n. 17/6, January 1971, p. 21.

artist, obtained a favorable response without much of an introduction, proof of the level of quality he achieved from the first. Moser presented his furniture for the first time at the Secession's eighth exhibit, the same occasion, as we have noted, of the arrival in Vienna of Mackintosh, Ashbee, and van de Velde. In a review of the show Bertha Zuckerkandl pointed out that Hoffmann's and Moser's furniture pieces were "architectonically developed in a clear and logical manner, adjusted to their function."[78] The same furniture was judged by Franz Servaes, the critic of the *Neue Freie Presse*, as being "totally devoid of affectation or of sophisticated torments."[79] And if Ludwig Hevesi had remembered his reference, in speaking of Moser, to "refined poetry," W. Fred in agreement (in a review in *Innen-Dekoration*) underlined that Moser could be considered the "most gifted" artist of the group.[80]

In this unanimous chorus Loos's opinion, stridently contrapuntal, is presented in his well-known *Ornament und Verbrechen* where he cites as an example of degeneration Moser's furniture at the eighth Secessionist exhibit.[81] This contrast in viewpoints is not merely fortuitous, but a symptom of an extreme polarity of opinion that existed within the criticism of furniture in general. Instead, however, the works of Moser and his colleagues were assumed to be precise cultural models. It is necessary meanwhile to reflect on the substantial intrinsic ambiguity of the work of the *Innenkünstler* (interior decorator) who, like Moser and so many others, was caught between the protagonists and the victims of a transition that was not only artistic but also cultural and commercial: it is almost superfluous to mention that these were the years of Art Nouveau and of the second industrial revolution.

Moser's active involvement as an interior decorator was too short and must be limited to the period of the first five years of the century in order to allow an easy delineation of the direction he took, of the stylistic and conceptual choices he made on projects (for example, the house of "Frau Dr. M." in 1902, and later the Stonborough House, 1905). As a comprehensive, albeit imperfect, image of Moser's intense although brief endeavor, we can consider one of his "reciprocal" friezes (the trout motif), *The Rich Catch of Fish* (shown in 1900), in which two strongly contrasting presences (white and black) and inverted symmetry generate a sequence throughout, while his motif, however much it advances, never changes.

It would be difficult to explain the reasons for the profound differences that separate two adjoining interiors in the same apartment without establishing some preliminary observations. In the first place Moser made a distinction, sometimes clearly and sometimes less so, between those interiors in a house that are used collectively and are open to those outside the family, and the more private spaces, which are removed from a wider usage and of a different symbolic status than the former; and those rooms that had a more functional usage, such as dressing rooms, corridors, bedrooms, boudoirs, and (obviously) the servants' quarters and kitchen.

It must be pointed out that Moser, probably more than Hoffmann, was

Bookshelves, part of an arrangement for "Frau Dr. M.," Vienna, 1903. (From *Das Interieur*, IV, 1903)

[78] B. Zuckerkandl, "Die erste Kunstgewerbe-Ausstellung des Sezession—I. Möbel," in *Wiener Allgemeine Zeitung*, 4 November 1900, cited in Schweiger, *Wiener Werkstätte*, p. 19.
[79] F. Servaes, "Kunst im Handwerk (Sezession)," in *Neue Freie Presse*, Vienna, 10 November 1900, cited in Schweiger, *Wiener Werkstätte*, p. 18.
[80] Hevesi, p. 289; Fred.
[81] A. Loos, *Ornament und Verbrechen*.

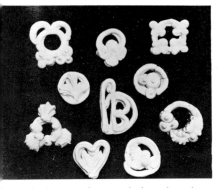

Bread shapes designed for the show "The Well-Set Table," organized in Vienna by the Wiener Werkstätte in 1906.

disarmed by the occasional confrontation with a client who would explicitly ask for an addition to the décor in order to flaunt it as a tangible symbol of wealth. In these cases, it must be said, Loos's moralizing hit the mark.

Two opposite tendencies engaged in a dialectic can be distinguished in the furniture and interiors designed by Moser; but in the background a constant element can be discerned. The first tendency can be defined as *purist*, as may be seen in Moser's house on the Hohe Warte; the second is the *graphic-decorative* tendency that is developed in the living room in the "House for a Young Couple."[82] The constant element is the *Biedermeier invariant*, which can be found either in the geometric simplicity of the purist designs or in the complex articulations of interiors governed by ornamental motifs; in fact, in these, the rigorous simplicity of the layout of the horizontal and vertical surfaces, and the recurrent simplicity of the volumes that comprise furniture and objects, are outstanding.

The Biedermeier style, as it was defined in those years by Joseph August Lux, a journalist friend of Hoffmann and Moser, was the style "of pure comfort in the simplicity of forms"; the term *Biedermeier* designated something which "originally did not belong to any style."[83] At the same time Zuckerkandl observed that it was either Hoffmann or Moser who had allowed that indigenous tradition to influence their projects "in order to give their work a national character."[84]

To the purist tendency belong, above all, the bright interiors of the Moser House on the Steifeldgasse 6, in the home built by Hoffmann on the Hohe Warte in 1902. These interiors allowed Moser to manipulate and shape in some way an architectural space not planned by him. At first they are not distinguishable from other contemporaneous and adjoining interiors designed by Hoffmann for the Henneberg and Spitzer Houses. In the Moser House, nevertheless, the built-in furniture and the tendency to arrange space on the horizontal predominate. This procedure, which recalls Mackintosh, was quite customary for Moser, who applied a constant quotient to his displays, decorations, and interior designs: a kind of functional moulding gave the space "the calm of a uniform height."[85]

In some interiors for the 1902 St. House and for "Frau Dr. M.'s" house in the same year, Moser used furniture that was lacquered or made of light natural wood and divided into square or rectangular modules in whose orthogonal order were framed, as a kind of counterpoint, the window panes and door panels, gracefully integrated and defined. In "Frau Dr. M.'s" dressing room Moser devised a system of storage spaces derived from a functional multi-purpose grid: the tray-like top of the dressing table, the tops of the low cabinets, and the handles of the high ones, as well as the height of the mirror and the overall order, were clearly based on a human scale.

This characteristic, in addition to the composition of the wall plan, forces the comparison with interiors that were done much later by Mogen Koch, Kaare Klint, or Gerrit Rietveld. More than similarity or kinship, there is a communality

[82] Zuckerkandl, *Koloman Moser.*
[83] J.A. Lux, "Villenkolonie Hohe Warte erbaut von Prof. Josef Hoffmann," in *Das Interieur*, IV, 1903, p. 129.
[84] Zuckerkandl, *Josef Hoffmann*, p. 6.
[85] Zuckerkandl, *Koloman Moser*, p. 333.

of sources, which for Moser was the Biedermeier tradition and for the others nineteenth century Scandinavian or Dutch tradition. These were formal systems among which there was much contact; this homogeneity had already been pointed out with illustrations in an article in *Hohe Warte* in 1906, where Biedermeier interior designs were compared to Dutch designs.[86]

With these projects as well as the interior décor for the house of "Dr. H." (1903) or other arrangements of domestic interiors for which only drawings and perspective sketches have remained, dated between 1902 and 1905, and in the absence of information about the client, Moser favored the development of what Zuckerkandl defined as *die tektoniche Richtung* (the techtonic trend) in the contemporary applied arts.[87] In this way Moser—who, after all, was a painter—strived to achieve an expertise as *Architecturentwerfer* (architectural planner), which he had been institutionally denied as he sanctioned the autonomy of interior design as a discipline with intrinsic artistic characteristics, qualities that, with his usual acumen, Renato De Fusco recently has suggested, are what "distinguish it from architecture by the fact that it utilizes the existing order of 'immobile' elements, integrating with another order, that of 'mobile' elements; while architecture shapes the entire spatial unity of a building, including the exterior, interior decoration is distinguishable in that its field of action is in the world of the single room."[88]

To the "tectonic" trend belong, for example, furniture pieces such as *Der reiche Fischzug*, the desk for the Wärndorfer House, the furniture planned for a showroom of the Böck porcelain factory, or finally the desk at the Stonborough House in Berlin. *Der reiche Fischzug*, executed by Portois & Fix in 1900 and exhibited at the eighth Secessionist show, is a credenza divided into three parts: a platform base with storage units, a writing section, and a top with a glass case. The main sections are differentiated through a volumetric play between concave and convex, where a recessed section is placed above; this almost complementary reciprocity between the cornices finds a perfect equivalence in the inlaid frieze, which is articulated vertically and based on a *reziproke Fischmotiv*— a design alternating black and white with reciprocal silhouettes of stylized fish. This was executed at least twice: one was bought, as we know, by the Minister of Culture, von Rittel, at the show; another was placed in the dining room of "Dr. Z.'s" house in 1903.[89]

The second tectonic example is a desk that Moser designed for an associate, Fritz Wärndorfer, around 1903. It was a prismatic, rather compact piece of furniture supported by tapering legs and incorporating a cubic seat. Once the seat is pulled out and the drop front is turned down, its function is disclosed: it is a *secrétaire* with an interior equipped with compartments and movable parts that open from the sides. Opening these lateral elements creates a microenvironment for the person using the desk, a sort of refuge that includes "interiority" within the space in which it is placed. One could compare this "furniture of wear" with a comfortable dressing gown because of the close relationship that it seems to establish between body and object. From this case,

Desk for the Stonborough House in Berlin, 1905.

[86] *Hohe Warte*, II, 1906-07, pp. 38-39.
[87] Zuckerkandl, *Koloman Moser*, p. 329.
[88] R. De Fusco, "Per una teoria dell'arredamento," in *Casa Vogue*, n. 150, March 1984, p. 199.
[89] This environment is illustrated in *Das Interieur*, IV, 1903, pp. 36-38.

Living room for Stonborough House in Berlin, 1905.

partial jewel box and partial stage set (but a stage set in reverse, with the "actor" looking *into* rather than *out* of it), Moser executed some variants: one for the "House for a Young Couple," and one for the Halle of the Palais Stoclet. But for its size and portability this piece of furniture provides a noteworthy comparison with the angular desk designed by Hoffmann for the Villa Spitzer around 1903. Moreover, Hoffmann's solution denies any sense of surprise and transformation in that it is fixed and completely closed, in contrast to Moser's magical and mysterious object, which holds the fascination of the old Biedermeier genius.[90]

Around 1902, Moser designed some furniture for the showroom of the Wiener Porzellanmanufaktur Jos. Böck, including two showcases and a table. The first two are made to provide a horizontal surface on which to display porcelain objects; the base, nonfunctional for display purposes, is closed by panels with concentric rectangular grooves enclosing an ellipsis; the shelves are held up by thin turned columns with a symmetrical capital for a base. All the surfaces are lacquered in white. The theme of "architectonic" furniture, in particular furniture using the column as a secondary structural element, was derived from nineteenth-century tradition; but for the furniture he designed for Böck, Moser probably looked to more recent models such as Voysey's of 1893, published in *The Studio*,[91] or a clock by Ashbee, published in *Innen-Dekoration* in 1899,[92] or, finally, a *Kästchen* (small box) for photographs designed by Olbrich around 1901. Naturally we are limited to the comparison of objects, however varied, that used the column motif in rather similar ways. Among Viennese designers the column was used rather frequently in the first years of the century, from some armoires and buffets designed by Wilhelm Schmidt for the Wiener Kunst im Hause in 1902, to a credenza placed by Hoffmann in the studio of the Spitzer House in 1903, to numerous clocks by Olbrich, Hoffmann, and Moser.

The graphic-decorative tendency that coexists peacefully with "architectural" furniture is on the whole free from pieces that present an analogous sense of order as well. This is the case of the desk at the Stonborough House in Berlin (1905), installed in collaboration with Hoffmann. The strong sculptural emphasis of this object is accentuated by the complete absence of decoration and visual accessorial elements such as footbase, frame, handles, etc. The desk is made up of two superimposed, asymmetrical, longitudinal volumes: a large one, a cubic base, on which rests a parallelepiped of the same depth but with a length one-and-a-half times the size of the base and half its height. A massive *T* is the configuration of the sides: the back is used for storage and the front as a desk whose writing shelf is obtained by opening out one of the panels of the upper unit. This distinction between base, upper parts, and overhanging cantilever forces into a precarious relationship two languages that, however interrelated, are quite distinct: the one of architectural planning, and the other of furniture design.

This desk manifests in many ways the basic limitations of Moser's concept of interior decoration. Moser was incapable of going beyond the materiality

[90] See the drawings of the collection of the Österreichisches Museum für angewandte Kunst, published in *Moderne Vergangenheit 1800-1900*, exhibition catalog, Künstlerhaus, Vienna, 1981, pp. 212-15.
[91] It concerns the "Cabinet for Lady Wentworth" of 1893. See *The Studio*, May 1896, p. 214.
[92] *Innen-Dekoration*, X, 1899, p. 219.

and static nature of an object if not through a pattern or a trellis, also asymmetrical, in which to arrange, respectively, a decoration or a set of functional elements. Incomparable in the creation of interiors and furniture or diaphanous objects, Moser found it difficult to connect tectonic imperatives to purist ones, however present, without resolving them into a synthesis as in this desk for the house of the lady in Berlin. It may be pointed out that this propensity to renounce ornamentation in preference for the basic stereometric forms is accentuated in the works that Moser executed with Hoffmann. Under these circumstances, Moser opted for a greater discretion, achieving a resultingly high quality.

In the absence of documentation it seems problematic, if not impossible, to delimit Hoffmann's responsibility from Moser's within a joint project, and it would be arbitrary to attribute the influence of one over the other in selected works or vice versa, in a work brought forth by both. One can speak plausibly of reciprocity, a closeness of the one to the other, resulting, as we have said several times, for the most part, in perfectly interchangeable contributions. This is the case, above all, in the interiors of the Purkersdorf Sanatorium, planned by Moser and consisting, as far as we know,[93] of the furniture for the rooms on the first floor, namely the music room, the smoking, and writing rooms. The piano, for example, is quite similar not only to a more "stripped down" version executed by the Gebrüder Stingl and based on Moser's plan,[94] but also to the "rich" variation placed by Hoffmann, about two years later, in the music room of the Palais Stoclet. The cubic armchairs of a living room in Hoffmann's Villa Spitzer, used, among other things, one of Moser's fabrics; but they are likewise similar to the model placed in front of the fireplace in H. Wittgenstein House; this model, as we have seen, which was until now attributed to Hoffmann, is in fact Moser's. This furniture, like the pieces done for the Halle (among which can be found the cubic armchair derived from one of Moser's models created for Prag-Rudniker and placed in the Klimt Room) raises questions about individual contribution; we will limit ourselves to pointing out that works executed in collaboration with two architects, such as the fashion salon of the sisters Flöge[95] and the Stonborough House,[96] presented an occasion for the two to achieve extremely modern results in the field of interior decoration, especially through the control and measure that govern their every gesture. It could be said that the most immediate and perceptible outcome of this joint labor was the suspension of the respective tensions of this experimental project, which thereby retrieved, it is worth saying, the tranquil geometry of the Biedermeier tradition.

We find other references than those from the start of the 19th century in the furniture of the Sanatorium, and even in the contemporary work of the Modern "masters"; in the living room at Stonborough House, the reference to tradition is explicit and is almost a historicist quote. The agile armchairs and the sofa have a wooden supporting structure with square sectional laths joining two fabrics and connected to the floor by an intermediary crosspiece:

[93] Levetus, *Modern Decorative Art in Austria*; Seckler, *Josef Hoffmann*, p. 288.
[94] Published in *Das Interieur*, IV, 1903, p. 46.
[95] For the fashion salon, Hoffmann furnished the office and the showroom, Moser the small salon. See Seckler, *Josef Hoffmann*, p. 290.
[96] Hoffmann furnished the dining room, the study, the guest and servants' rooms; Moser furnished the living room and the *Toilettenzimmer*. See Seckler, *Josef Hoffmann*, p. 292.

Detail of decoration design for the Sacred Heart Church at Düsseldorf. (From *Deutsche Kunst und Dekoration*, n. 24, 1909)

the entire base is inscribable by a rhombus and is in trapezoidal sections. The seats, other than the horizontal piano seat, have three levels of slightly flaring padding; the seat back is higher than the sides and slightly pointed. If we omit the straightening of almost all curved lines and the use of batik fabric, we could equally well apply this description equally to the Biedermeier divans in vogue in Austria around 1825.[97]

Another of Moser's perfectly balanced interiors that dates back to tradition and the modern purist requirements may be found in the living room for Broncia and Hugo Koller in Vienna (1905). One can say that the whole room was structured around a regulating motif, an ellipsis that circumscribed a narrow rhombus (with curves symmetrical to the external one) and was itself inscribed by a rectangle. The marked tectonic accent and the heightened structural purity of the furniture is alleviated by this ornamental motif used by Moser as a conceptual device, a kind of modular path. In fact, with the exception of the backs of the chair and armchair where the elliptical design functions as a visual coordinating element, the module—used for its height and size—sets the scale for the furniture on its three axes, from the sofa to the showcase, from the bookshelf to the desk.

Describing this interior, Bertha Zuckerkandl underlined that Moser, under the circumstances, had manifested "a tendency toward purity of line, a yearning for aristocratic proportions, the search for structural meaning, the elimination of the superornate, the love for simple shapes, the inclination toward symmetrical structures."[98] The interiors of the Koller House, then, could be seen as a representative of Moser's entire production, especially for the clear equilibrium between tendencies that more than once contradict each other—namely, the "purist" and the "graphic-decorative." But one could add that this furniture better exemplified the functionalist aesthetic proposed by Hoffmann in his well-known *Einfache Möbel*, 1901, than did the illustrations used by Hoffmann in his article. Moser's furniture, in this case, seems to fit to perfection all the characteristics that, according to Hoffmann, should be integral to a proper plan, from the structural authenticity to the use of natural wood, stained but not painted (if now white), to the elimination of decoration as a mere cosmetic element used to distinguish movable furniture from that built into the wall.

Otherwise, Moser specified that decorated furniture should be strictly mimetic of its spatial surroundings. His imagination, as we shall soon see, was intensely concentrated on the idea of a *scene* in its etymological meaning of shadow, a place of fluid lines that seem to evoke the unearthly, an incomparably nocturnal space. At times the decoration seems too obsessive and close to the perversity of *trompel'oeil*, capable of swallowing up reality. In these cases—and if I understand it, in a perspective quite removed from the illuministic one of the Modern movement—Moser seems intent on designing uninhabitable houses for nonexistent people.

Moser's Art of the Room

Around 1906 the Werkstätte's activity became, according to Moser, "too diver-

[97] See *Moderne Vergangenheit*, in particular the photographs numbered 39, 41 and 42, 122, 126; and Baroni and D'Auria, 1981, photograph on p. 31.
[98] Quoted in W.J. Schweiger, author of an annotated index for the set, in *Moderne Vergangenheit*, p. 290.

sified, multiform and too dependent on the taste of the clients. Moreover, the public often doesn't know what it wants." "It was the impossible demands of the clientele," continues Moser, "and other divergent opinions which induced me to leave the Wiener Werkstätte several years ago."[99]

The "other divergent" opinions concerned the administrative growth and the increasingly complex management of the enterprise. Moser, immediately aware that the cost of quality products would necessarily be very high, wanted the Werkstätte to work only under commission.[100] But even when this condition was met, the resulting balance was not satisfactory, and the direct proportion between existing funds, provisions, and expenses for the realization of projects brought the whole enterprise to the brink of ruin; the instance of the most important project of the Werkstätte, the Palais Stoclet, comes to mind. Moser was aware that the production costs would not be easily covered by acceptable prices: "Nobody can live with this system, as long as he does not work for his descendants."[101]

In this light, the project that Moser executed around 1904 in Berlin, for a "young couple," appears emblematic. This interior décor, which as we have seen was amply illustrated and described, was articulated in all the rooms of a big apartment that included salons, waiting and dining rooms, studio, boudoir, bedrooms, dressing rooms, servants' quarters, bathrooms, kitchen, and so on. Bertha Zuckerkandl, with a phrase that to us today may sound ironic, emphatically declared that in that house everything was "predisposed to last for centuries, like the furniture of our ancestors."[102]

Everything in this interior was tangibly sumptuous. The finest woods and costliest materials, from ebony to coral, from mother-of-pearl to ivory, were methodically lavished on all the surfaces of the decorative modules in a consistent rhythm. In the living room all the furniture was regulated by a square module ten centimeters long; multiplying itself, inverting, subdividing and reversing itself, this quadrangle generated density, height, and depth. On the walls, to balance so much obsessive stereometric orthogonality, there was a broad floral pattern. In the dining room Moser transferred the decorative scansion to the walls and ceiling; the pattern, rough plaster flowers in gold, emerged above the "functional level" determined by the fittings and joined the ceiling to converge toward its center, from which hung three groups of bell-shaped lamps: almost a three-dimensional version of the decoration used on the surfaces throughout.

In the *Frühstückszimmer*—literally the "breakfast room," but resembling a boudoir—the decorative module, vaguely phytomorphic, set the scale for the furniture, determining through their transformation and multiplication their size and functional role. In this case one can speak, more than ever, of a *decorational module*, in the manifest aesthetic pleasure sought either through ornamentation or through satisfying structural or functional demands.

Zuckerkandl spoke of "ornamental abstraction" and did not fail to stress that "the ornament as an end in itself is for Moser a secondary consideration. When the feeling and the functional sense of a space require or justify ornamentation, Moser would use it with concern only for the structural conditions...

Desk for the Wärndorfer House, Vienna, 1903. (Museum für angewandte Kunst, Vienna)

[99] Moser, p. 11.
[100] This attitude is referred to by Mackintosh, who subscribes to it in a letter to Wärndorfer in 1903; cited in Schweiger, *Wiener Werkstätte*, p. 23.
[101] A letter by Moser to Hoffmann in February 1907; cited in Schweiger, *Wiener Werkstätte*, p. 68.
[102] Zuckerkandl, *Koloman Moser*, p. 340.

The mixture of rigorous Sachlichkeit and refined spiritual beauty make up the artist's most remarkable characteristics."[103]

The duality of Moser's poetics—that is, the dialectic tension between decorative graphics and purist functionalism, between ornamental and structural patterns—emerges again. But were we to consider the recently discussed living room furniture stripped of all decoration, we would find an example of the *konstruktive Forderung* (the structural exigency) used to show up the other, however manifestly expressed.

But what is the complex meaning of Moser's interior decoration, his concept of the *art of interior space?* "If the room is elevated to the level of art, if the creation of aesthetic value is attempted," wrote Muthesius of Mackintosh's projects, "it is only because it is right to create perfection."[104] That then, continued the German critic, this conception would become misappropriated in the cultural milieu of prospective clients is another story. "People today, especially men in their work spaces, are strangers in this magical fairy-tale world."[105] The art of interior space should, then, take the road between the "rooms for spectres" of the Scottish group, and the interiors generated exclusively by the Sachlichkeit.

Moser tried to weld together magic and reason, dream and necessity: he brought to focus a very special concept of *Raumkunst* (interior decoration) not so different, in any case, from Mackintosh's and more than once connected to Olbrich's and Hoffmann's; that synthesizing space consisted in freeing it from the constrictions of the enveloping building, from the fixity of its contours. The stage sets of the *Stilbühne* (stylized theatre) of 1901, the numerous installations of art shows and design exhibits, the windows for Steinhof, and the decorations for the Church of the Sacred Heart in Düsseldorf[106] can be viewed as testimony, with the many "domestic" interiors, of the same uninterrupted pursuit: the creation of spaces that would evoke an atmosphere rather than merely provide parameters and functions, in which there would be "active" values other than the almost immanent, and at times authoritarian, presence of architecture. From this perspective Moser's most exemplary projects turned out to be two installations for Klimt's paintings; the first at the 18th Secessionist exhibition in 1903, the second at the Kunstschau in 1908. The 1903 show was arranged in large white rooms; in the main ones were hung the two large canvases, *Philosophy* and *Medicine*, that Klimt had painted for the large hall at the University of Vienna. The white "cubic" chairs—single, thin presences that were not square—were well-spaced from each other. The vertical planes, corresponding in every edge and intersection with the horizontal planes, were defined by rectangular motifs in black and white, arranged in an implied grid pattern, which thus integrated the wall to the paintings, becoming their passepartout. From the translucent ceiling hung four global lamps. Looking at the few photographs of this installation, another function that Moser must have assigned to the chairs emerges: that of a dimensional counterpoint to the out-of-scale figures in the paintings, which, given their original commission, had

103 Ibid.
104 Muthesius, *Das englische Haus*, English translation, p. 52.
105 Ibid.
106 K. Moser, "Koloman Mosers Projekt für die Ausmalung der Heil—Geist-Kirche in Düsseldorf," in *Deutsche Kunst und Dekoration*, XII, 1909, pp. 347-52.

gigantic dimensions.

In an adjacent room where studies and sketches hung, Moser delimited the visual field by lowering the horizontal margin of the walls to approximately two meters from the ground. The white chairs of the previous room gave way to a chair with arms and straw seat, designed for Prag-Rudniker. To set the scale of the exhibition space by relating the smallest pieces to the largest, and to set actual limits on the proper distance to view the drawings, Moser introduced high, narrow flower boxes that discretely defined those zones to be used for contemplative pauses and those to be used as passages. Because of this installation, many who commented enthusiastically, hailed Moser as the "incomparable director of art exhibit installations"[107] and creator of exemplary environments "determined by the modern technique of the exhibition."[108]

In the Klimt Room installed for the Kunstschau in 1908, Moser, as Fanelli has written, "proposed a version of his installations based on the isolated dot element distributed according to an amplied modular grid."[109] For this extremely refined *Raumkunst* exercise for which, for once, the decoration invents an architectonic space, the graphico-decorative—more than ever *deco-rational*—passes into a functional constructive role; in this way any suspicion of playful frivolity (as connotative of formal surplus—even that label, "Viennese," is too quickly attributed to Moser) is finally removed from decoration.

In the Klimt Room of 1908 the most successful synthesis of Moser's two fundamental needs is achieved: graphics and purism coincide, and the *feeling* of the architectural space is obtained and communicated through expressive means reduced to the minumum. And the stage setting succeeds by virtue of the reductive rule that seems to govern it, because of the supreme control that converts an interior into an almost intangible spaciality signaled only by intermittent graphics, in a *painted* image of the interior, and because of this very idea became historical. Nevertheless the deletion of a historicity that was perceived as deleterious was possibly Moser's most authentic point of tension. In this, one of his last *Raumkunst* works, he came close, fascinated and terrified at once, to the ground zero of his work.

The calibrated prefiguration of the silence that Moser was soon to choose for himself and the discomfort of an attitude that measures and demolishes the limits of *Innendekoration* are concentrated in a room that paradoxically might be taken as a model of the Modern movement.

[107] Zuckerkandl, *Koloman Moser*, p. 341.
[108] This comment of Julius Meier-Graefe appeared in 1904; see Schweiger, *Wiener Werkstätte*, p. 13.
[109] Fanelli and Godoli, p. 111.

Restaurant of the Hotel Bristol at Warsaw by Otto Wagner, with window by Moser, 1902.

Window for the Hotel Bristol.

Vignettes for *Ver Sacrum*, 1898-99.

Summer, illustration for the *Allegorien* of the Gerlach publishing house, Vienna, 1895.

Frieze for *Allegorien*, 1895.

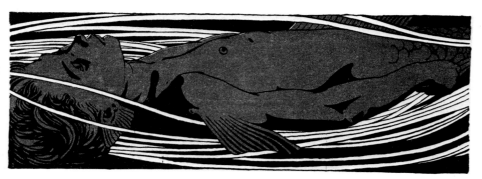

Hunting and Fishing—Water Sports—Bicycling, a plate from *Allegorien*, 1895.

Head of a Girl, 1900. (Collection J. Hummel, Vienna)

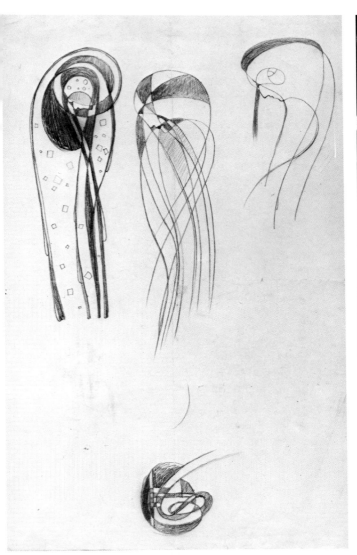

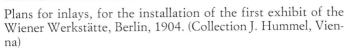

Plans for inlays, for the installation of the first exhibit of the Wiener Werkstätte, Berlin, 1904. (Collection J. Hummel, Vienna)

Study for calendar, ca. 1901. (Private Collection, Vienna)

Ondine, woodcut, 1902. (Collection J. Hummel, Vienna)

Left:
February, calendar page, 1901. (Collection J. Hummel, Vienna)

Right:
Poster for the *Jung-Wiener Theater zum lieben Augustin*. (From *Die Fläche*, n. 1, 1901)

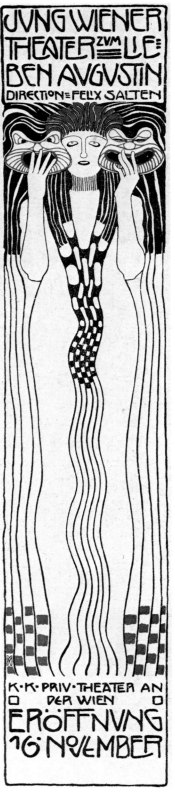

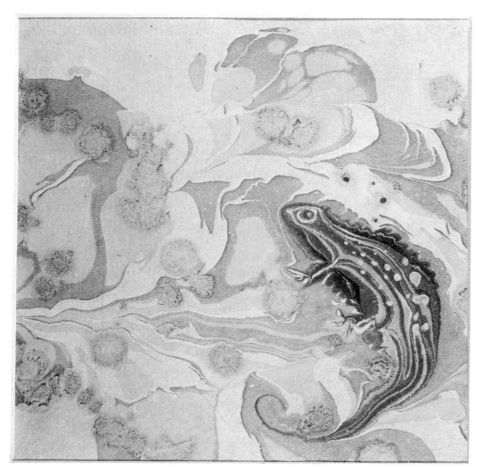

Three ornamental motifs using the technique of marbleized paper, 1904. (Collection J. Hummel, Vienna)

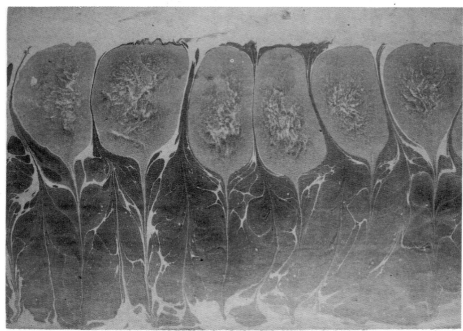

Head of a girl, published in *Ver Sacrum*, n. 1, 1898. (Collection J. Hummel, Vienna)

Sieben Billionen Jahre vor meiner Geburt
war ich eine Schwertlilie.

Unter meinen schimmernden Wurzeln
drehte sich
ein andrer Stern.

Auf seinem dunklen Wasser
schwamm
meineblaue Riesenblüte.

Drawing for a page in *Ver Sacrum*, n. 11, 1898. (Collection J. Hummel, Vienna)

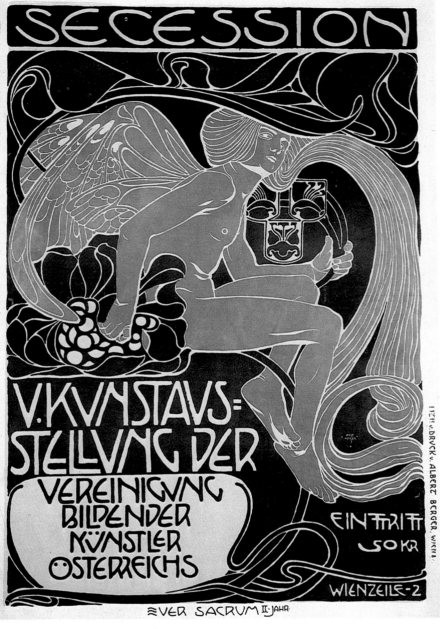

Poster for the Secession's Show V, 1899.

Poster for the Secession's Show XIII, 1902. (From *Ver Sacrum*, n. 6, 1902)

VER
SACRVM

Poster for *Fromme's Kalender*. (From *Die Fläche*, n. 1, 1901)

Preceding page, from top left:
Drawing for cover of *Ver Sacrum*, 1898. (Collection J. Hummel, Vienna)

Plan for illustration for *Ver Sacrum*, n. 2, 1898. (Private Collection, Vienna)

Plan for calendar, *July*, published in *Ver Sacrum*, n. 1, 1901. (Collection J. Hummel, Vienna)

Two pages for a text by Rainer Maria Rilke. (From *Ver Sacrum*, n. 21, 1901)

Poster for J. & J. Kohn for the Russian market, 1903. (Historisches Museum der Stadt Wien, Vienna)

Poster for use within the Wiener Werkstätte, ca. 1904.

Poster for use within the Wiener Werkstätte, ca. 1904.

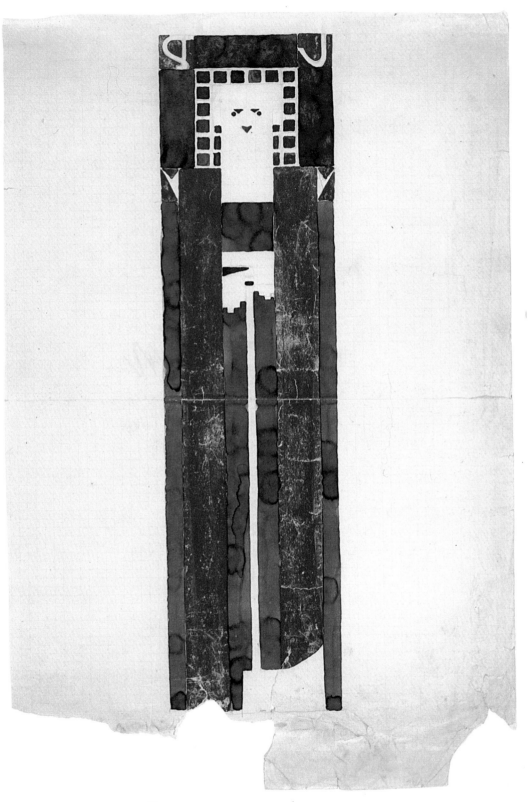

Plan for a window for the Steinhof Church, 1905. (Collection J. Hummel, Vienna)

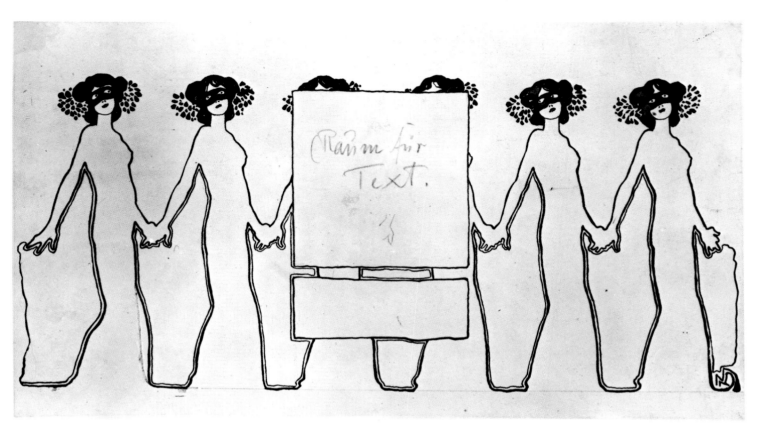

Study of a graphic frieze for *Ver Sacrum*, 1898. (Private Collection, Vienna)

Drawing, ca. 1903. (Private Collection, Vienna)

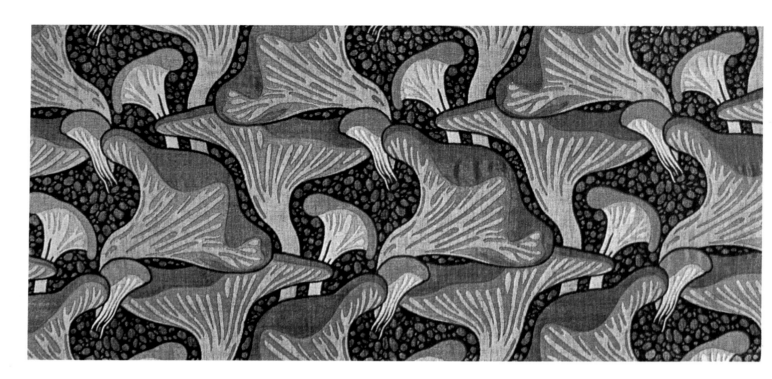

Fabric design for Backhausen, 1902.

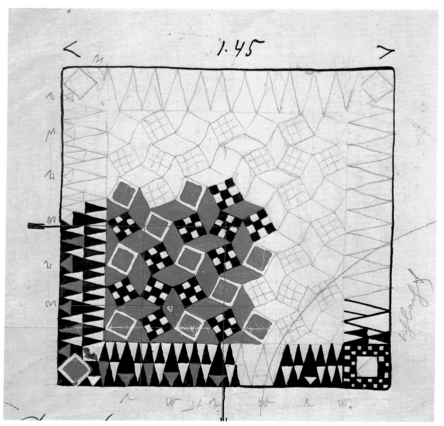

Plan for a carpet for Backhausen, placed by Moser in the boudoir of "Frau Dr. M.," Vienna, 1903.

Study for wallpaper, *Waves of the Danube*, for *Flächenschmuck*, 1901. (Museum für angewandte Kunst, Vienna)

Ornamental motif, *Reciprocal Ballerinas*, for *Flächenschmuck*, 1901.

Postcard for Franz Joseph's Jubilee, 1908.

Sketch for a commemorative stamp, ca. 1908. (Museum für angewandte Kunst, Vienna)

Opposite:
Frieze and letter heading for a page of the commemorative volume *Die K.K. Hof und Staatsdruckerei, 1804-1904* (with woodcut by O. Czeschka).

ROTATIONS=
MASCHINEN
F·Ü·R·E·I·N·
UND·ZWEI=
F·A·R·B·E·N·
D·R·U·C·K

Bei einer Beurteilung der graphisch-technischen Leistungen der Staats-druckerei ist es nur natürlich, wenn dem Buchdruck der breiteste Raum zugewiesen wird. Nicht allein seine kulturelle Bedeutung, welche den Charakter der von uns „Neuzeit" ge-nannten geschichtlichen Epoche weit-aus mehr zu beeinflussen bestimmt war, als es die Entdeckung Amerikas vermochte, ist hiefür maßgebend, sondern auch der Umstand, daß der Buchdruck als die Mutterkunst aller übrigen graphischen Fächer anzusehen ist, und endlich die Tatsache, daß ihm vor allem andern der größte Anteil an der Beschaffung der für die verschiedensten Bedürfnisse auf allen Gebieten des staat-lichen, gesellschaftlichen und geschäftlichen Lebens notwendigen Druckwerke zukommt. Die außerordentlichen Verdienste, welche sich unser Staatsinstitut vornehmlich in der Sphäre des Buchdrucks erworben hat, sind von weit über die heimischen Grenzen ragender Bedeutung. Die Anstalt beschränkte sich nicht allein darauf, dem

Windows over the main entrance of the Steinhof Church by Otto Wagner, 1904-08.

Cartoons for a detail for the window *Eternal Father*, Steinhof Church, showing *Adam and Eve* and *Fish and Birds*, 1905. (Collection J. Hummel, Vienna)

Cartoon for a window for the Steinhof Church, *Angels*, 1905. (Private Collection, Vienna)

Cartoon for the window *Eternal Father*, Steinhof Church, 1905. (Private Collection, Vienna)

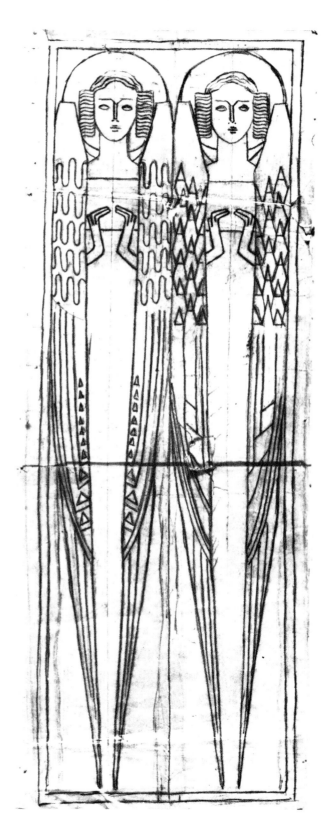

Plan for embossed metal for a desk, 1904. (Collection J. Hummel, Vienna)

Opposite:
Plan for a window, ca. 1904. (Private Collection, Vienna)

Adam and *Eve* cartoons for the windows of the Steinhof Church, ca. 1905.
(Private Collection, Vienna)

KOLOMAN MOSER

Stage set for the comedy *Jeppe von Berge* by L. Holbergs, 1912. (Private Collection, Vienna)

Study for the decoration of the altar of the Steinhof Church, 1905-06. (Collection J.Hummel, Vienna)

Preceding page: Almanac of the Wiener Werkstätte with costume for the ballerina Miss George, 1910. (Private Collection, Vienna)

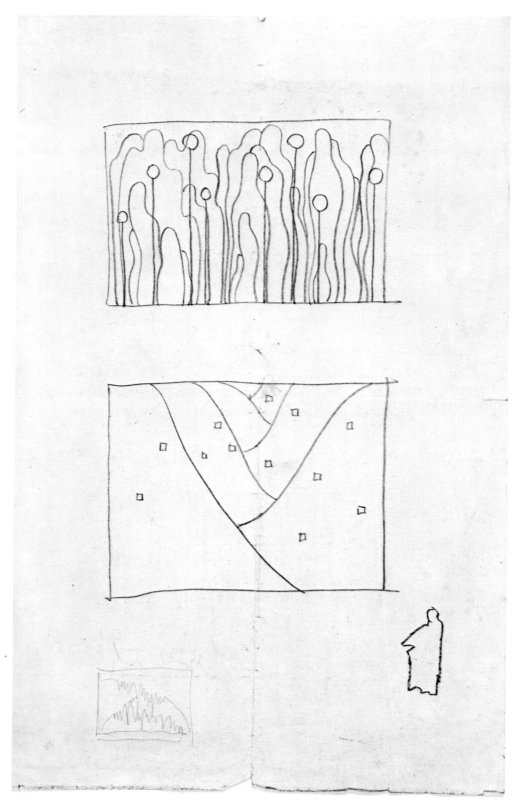

Sketch for the stage set for *Der Bergsee* by Julius Bittner, 1910. (Collection J. Hummel, Vienna)

Opposite:
Woman, oil on canvas, ca. 1910. (Collection J. Hummel, Vienna)

From left:
Woman with Hat, oil on canvas, 1893.
(Hochschule für angewandte Kunst,
Vienna)
Self-Portrait as a Young Man, oil on canvas, ca. 1893. (Hochschule für angewandte Kunst, Vienna)

Pietà, oil on canvas, 1896. (Collection J. Hummel, Vienna)

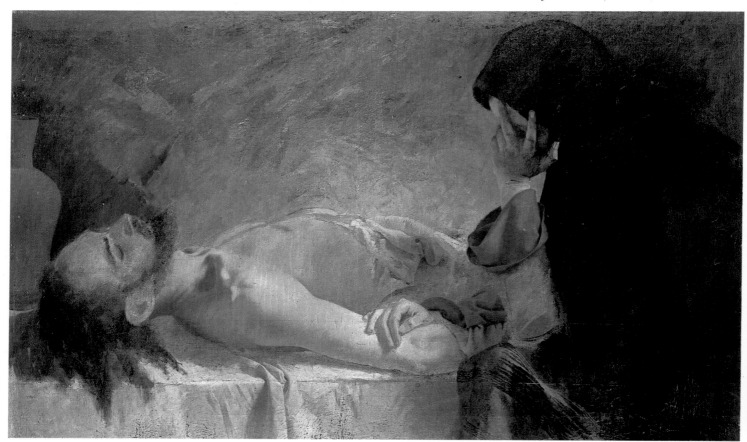

Wolfgangsee, oil on canvas, 1913. (Collection J. Hummel, Vienna)

From left:
Recto of a page in the album *Flächenschmuck* (plate 5), 1901.
Plan for the inlays for the credenza *The Rich Catch of Fish*, and study for typographical characters, 1900. (Hochschule für angewandte Kunst, Vienna)

Pattern design, ca. 1902. (Private Collection, Vienna)

Pattern plan, 1899. (Collection J. Hummel, Vienna)

Three Crouching Women, oil on canvas, ca. 1914. (Museum Moderner Kunst, Vienna)

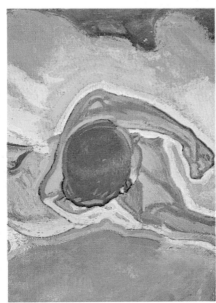

Preceding page, from top left:
Flowers in Garden, oil on canvas, 1909. (Private Collection, Vienna)
Semmering, oil on canvas, ca. 1912. (Private Collection, Vienna)
Still Life with Fruit, oil on canvas, 1910. (Private Collection, Vienna)
Study for *The Wayfarer*, oil on canvas, 1916. (Collection J. Hummel, Vienna)

Light, oil on canvas, 1913. (Collection J. Hummel, Vienna)

Tile embossed in copper, 1903-04. (Historisches Museum der Stadt Wien, Vienna)

Bottom left: Small perfume bottle, 1904-05. (Collection J. Hummel, Vienna)

Plan for a ciborium, ca. 1905.

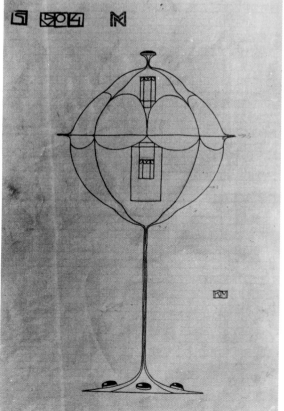

Glass in colored crystal, ca. 1900.

Small glass panel for a credenza, 1902. (Collection J. Hummel, Vienna)

Opposite: *Susanna and the Two Elders*, tempera, 1916. (Collection J. Hummel, Vienna)

Desk set in cut metal, executed at Wiener Werkstätte, 1904-05. (Collection J. Hummel, Vienna)

Flower vases in cut metal, executed at Wiener Werkstätte, 1904-05.

Ciborium in silver and semiprecious stones, executed at Wiener Werkstätte, ca. 1905.

Top left: Sugar bowl (attributed to Moser), ca. 1905. (Collection J. Hummel, Vienna)

Bottom left: Wastepaper basket in cut metal, executed by Wiener Werkstätte, 1904. (Collection J. Hummel, Vienna)

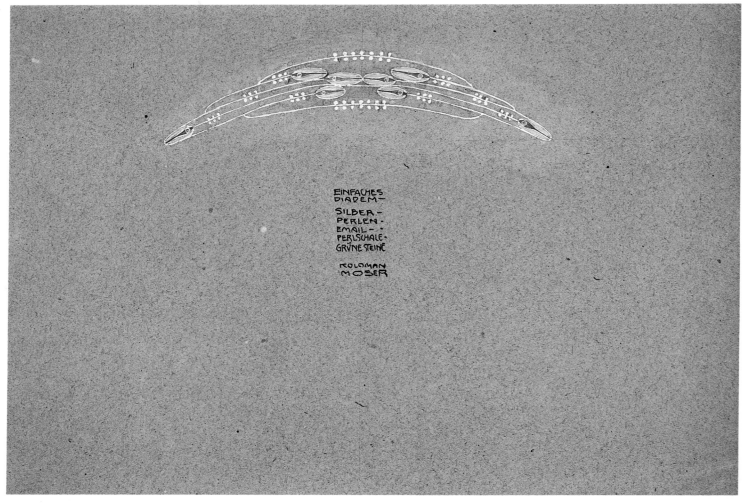

Plan for a silver diadem, 1902. (Collection J. Hummel, Vienna)

Plan for a wastepaper basket in silver and semiprecious stones, 1905. (Museum für angewandte Kunst, Vienna)

Plan for a necklace, ca. 1905. (Museum für angewandte Kunst, Vienna)

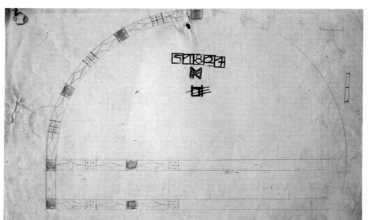

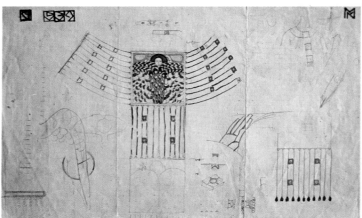

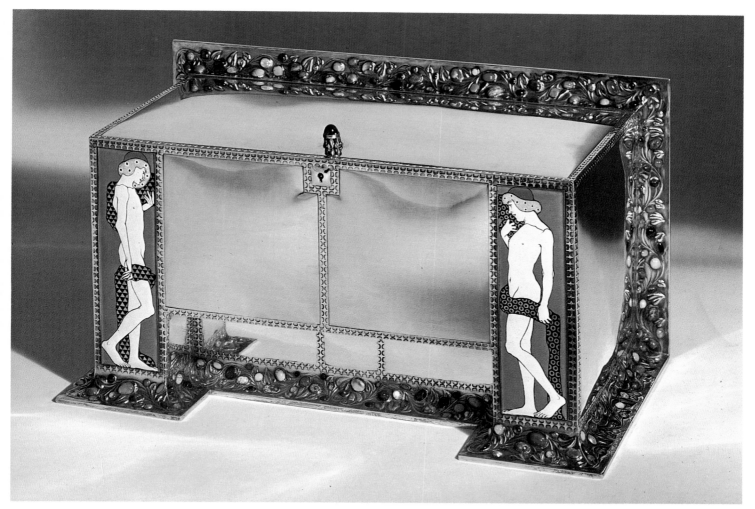

Silver box embossed with semiprecious stones, executed at the Wiener Werkstätte, 1906. (Museum für angewandte Kunst, Vienna)

Two plans for clocks, ca. 1905. (Museum für angewandte Kunst, Vienna)

Clock embossed in metal. (From *Deutsche Kunst und Dekoration*, n. 24, 1909-10)

Chair in bent beechwood, executed by Kohn, 1901. (Collection J. Hummel, Vienna)

Credenza executed by Kohn, 1902. (Collection J. Hummel, Vienna)

Plan for a bookshelf, 1910. (Museum für angewandte Kunst, Vienna)

Chair executed by Prag-Rudniker, 1902-03. (Collection J. Hummel, Vienna)

J. Hoffmann and K. Moser, the Hall at the Purkersdorf Sanatorium, 1903-05.

Flower stand (attributed to Moser), 1903-04. (Collection J. Hummel, Vienna)

Two hanging lamps in crystal and brass, ca. 1902. (Collection J. Hummel, Vienna)

Crystal vase, ca. 1903. (Collection J. Hummel, Vienna)   Glasses, ca. 1903. (Collection J. Hummel, Vienna)

Bowls and flower vases in crystal (in collaboration with R. Holubetz), 1901. (Collection J. Hummel, Vienna)

Blumenglas

flower glasses

Blumenglas
flower glass

glas für Gold-fische

Bowl for gold fish

Signum aufgeätzt.
J. Bakalowitz
& Söhne – Wien

Koloman Moser. Executed by J. Bakalowitz & Sons, Vienna.

Crystal vases produced by Bakalowits, ca. 1900.

Crystal vase produced by Bakalowits, ca. 1900. (Collection J. Hummel, Vienna)

Vase produced by Bakalowits, ca. 1900. (Collection J. Hummel, Vienna)

Bottle produced by Bakalowits, ca. 1900. (Collection J. Hummel, Vienna)

Plan for a living room interior, ca. 1903. (Collection J. Hummel, Vienna)

Plan for a wall installation, ca. 1903. (Collection J. Hummel, Vienna)

Plan for a carpet, 1901. (Collection J. Hummel, Vienna)

Jutta Sika (*Moserschule*), coffee set, produced by Böck, 1902.

Vase in colored glass and copper (*Moserschule*), 1900.

Ceramic vases, ca. 1900.

Ceramic vase, ca. 1900. (Collection J. Hummel, Vienna)

111

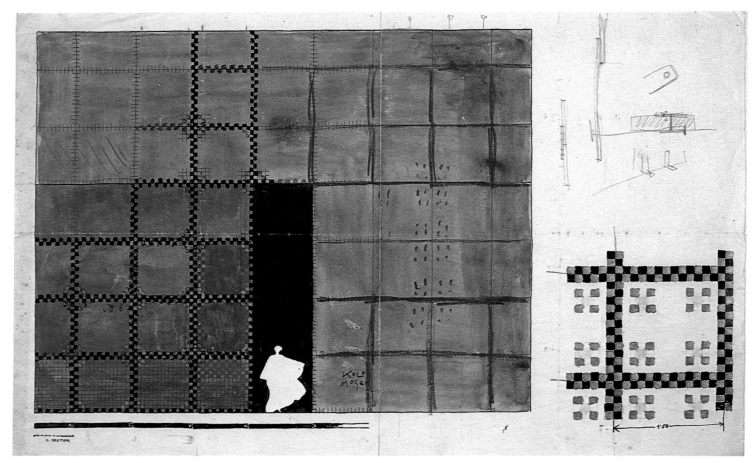

Sketch for a stage set, ca. 1901. (Collection J. Hummel, Vienna)

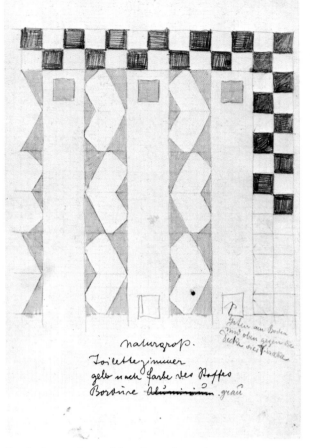

Plan for wall decorations for an apartment in Berlin, ca. 1903. (Collection J. Hummel, Vienna)

Study for a piece of furniture for a dressing room, ca. 1904. (Hochschule für angewandte Kunst, Vienna)

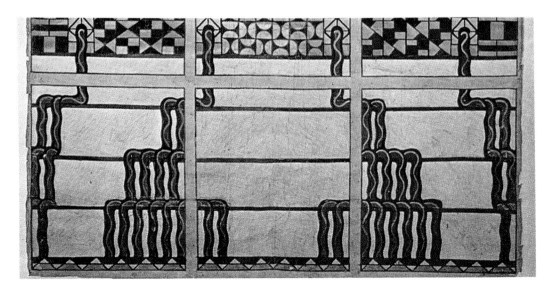

Detail for the window *Eternal Father*, Steinhof Church, 1905. (Private Collection, Vienna)

Plan for a bedroom, view of
two walls, ca. 1901. (Hochschule für angewandte Kunst,
Vienna)

FENSTER

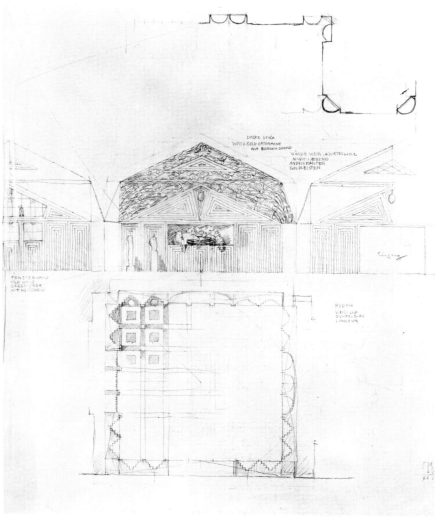

From left:
J. Hoffmann and K. Moser, arrangement for the fashion salon of the two Flöge sisters, Vienna, 1904. Plan for an installation, probably for an exhibit, ca. 1905. (Private Collection, Vienna)

Cover for an issue of *Ver Sacrum* dedicated to Arno Holz, 1901.

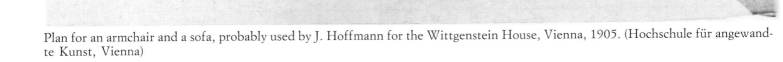

J/136

1:20.

1:10.

Nº 79.

KM

Plan for an armchair and a sofa, probably used by J. Hoffmann for the Wittgenstein House, Vienna, 1905. (Hochschule für angewandte Kunst, Vienna)

Chair executed by Prag-Rudniker, 1903. (Collection J. Hummel, Vienna)

Footstool executed by Kohn, ca. 1901. (Collection J. Hummel, Vienna)

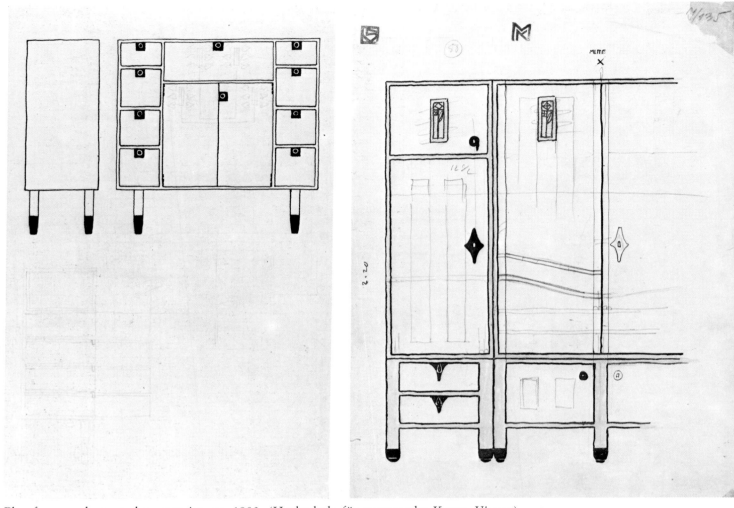

Plan for a credenza and an armoire, ca. 1903. (Hochschule für angewandte Kunst, Vienna)

Graphic margin frames for an issue of *Ver Sacrum* dedicated to Arno Holz, n. 18, 1901.

Prolog.

Seit der alte Papa Wieland
seine liederlichen Musen
abenteuerlich ersuchte,
ihm den Hippogryph zu satteln,
hat schon mancher deutsche Dichter
diesen Tric ihm nachgeäfft.

In das süsse blaue Wunder
unsrer Jungfer Poesie
stippte altklug Mutter Prosa
die didaktisch lange Nase,
und die Töchter des Olympiers
degradirt nun frech zu Jockeys
jeder Schlingel, dem erbärmlich
auf der schlechtgeleimten Leier
nur ein dünnes Därmchen schnurrt.

Ich = bin leider auch nur Mensch.

Dumpf in meine Wiegenlieder
brandete von fern die Ostsee,
und wir Deutschen sind entweder
Dichter oder Philosophen.

Ich bin Dichter. Versefex.

Versefex und degradir drum
jene schlanken Marmorschönen
mit den weltverliebten Herzen
heute selbst zum Stallknechtsdienst.

He, Euterpe, raus den Schinder!
Wiehernd bäumt er sich ins Licht.

Sie, Urania! erstmal, bitte,
dort den Strohhalm aus dem Schwanz.

Weint er unterm Baume Bo,
haha, hehe, hihi, hoho!

Pickelhering.

Träumt er abends unter Rüstern,
fühlt er, wie sie ihm umdüstern.

Streckt sich die Chaussee mit Pappeln,
fängts ihn schliesslich an zu rappeln.

Knüpft er sich an eine Weide,
singt er schluchzend noch: ich scheide.

Alle.

Sechs Bretter, fein gefugt aus Fichten,
endlich hört er auf zu dichten!

Schuh- und Versfaiseur Hans Sachs =
Horribiliscribifax!

Das böse Gewissen.

Was ist ein Dichter ohne Reim?
ein todter Tischler ohne Leim.

Schon klingt es mir im Ohre:
Anch'io son pittore!

Die Alten.

Drum lausche, wies im Winde weht,
der Blume Blühn ist ihr Gebet;
du hörst nur, wie das Herz dir klopft
und wie der Thau von den Rosen tropft!

Sonderling.

Nur selten komm ich aus dem Haus,
die Welt sieht so japanisch aus.

Ein Herr Anfang Zwanzig.

Ich kann und mag ihn nicht mehr dämpfen,
mir aus dem Herzen bricht der Schrei:
auf Tod und Leben lass uns kämpfen,
du legitime Tyrannei!
An deine windigen Tiraden
häng ich dies bleierne Gewicht:
das Volk nur ist von Gottes Gnaden,
sein König aber ist es nicht!

Mir presst das Herz, mir schnürts die Kehle,
und krampfhaft ballt sich mir die Faust,
wenn du im Schmuck der Kronjuwele
nur Kirchen und Kasernen baust.
Der Freiheit gibst du Bastonnaden,
der Wahrheit speihst du ins Gesicht:
das Volk nur ist von Gottes Gnaden,
sein König aber ist es nicht!

Ein Herr Mitte Dreissig.

Hilfe, mir platzt das Trommelfell!
Was hat den Kerl gestochen?
Um Gotteswillen, schnell, nur schnell!
er kommt sonst in die Wochen.
Ihn ärgerts, dass die Welt sich dreht.
Schimpft drauf, druckts und nennt sich = Poet!

Pickelhering.

Es fällt der Schnee in dicken Flocken,
die Menschheit kann ihn nicht mehr locken;
idyllisch lauscht er auf die Chöre
der Aepfel in der Ofenröhre.

Drop-front desk with matching chair for the Stoclet Palace, ca. 1906.

Chair for the boudoir of the "House for a Young Couple," 1903-04. (Private Collection, Vienna)

Plan for a tapestry, 1904-05.

Preceding page, from top left:
Study for the inlay for the credenza *The Rich Catch of Fish*, 1900.
The Rich Catch of Fish, exhibited at the Secession Exposition VIII, 1900.
Desk, ca. 1902. (From *Das Interieur*, IV, 1903)

Credenza executed by Ungenthüm, probably after Moser's design, 1900. The inlaid frieze is identical to the one Moser designed for a fabric in 1899.

Opposite: Ornamental motifs published in *Ver Sacrum* in 1899.

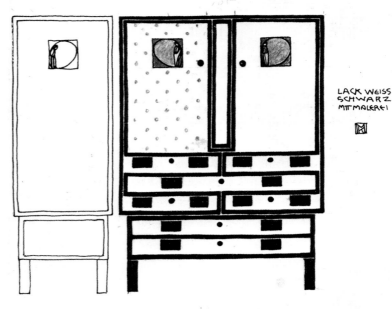

LACK WEISS
SCHWARZ
MIT MALEREI

Design for fabric pattern, 1899. (Hochschule für angewand-te Kunst, Vienna)

Design for lacquered furniture with painted inserts, 1903. (Collection J. Hummel, Vienna)

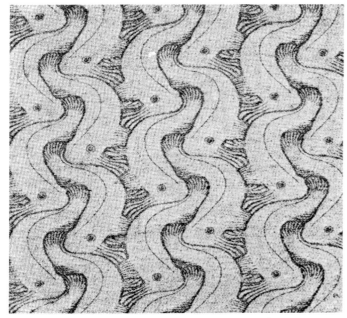

Opposite: Plan for wallpaper, ca. 1903. (Collection J. Hummel, Vienna)

Fabric made by Backhausen, 1899.

Display stand and table for the showroom of the Böck Factory, 1902. (Collection J. Hummel, Vienna)

Lacquered table, executed by Wiener Werkstätte, ca. 1904. (Collection J. Hummel, Vienna)

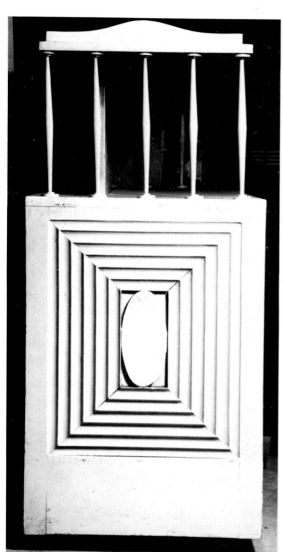

Side view of showcase for Böck products.

Lacquered armoire (sometimes attributed to Hoffmann and sometimes to Moser), ca. 1904. (Collection J. Hummel, Vienna)

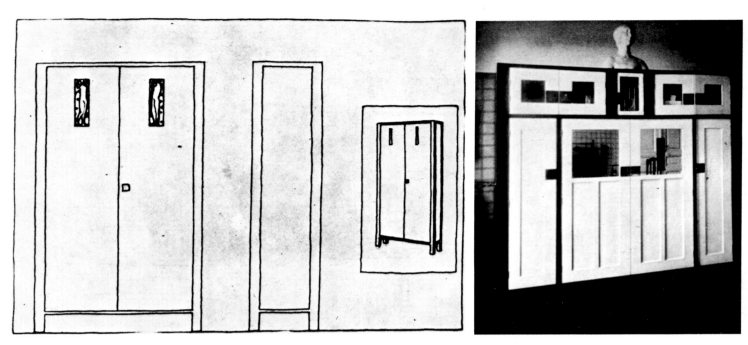

Chest of drawers from the Moser House, 1902. (Collection J. Hummel, Vienna)

Preceding page, from top left:
Plan for a closet, 1903. (Private Collection, Vienna)
Furniture for the bedroom of "Frau Dr. M." (From *Das Interieur*, IV, 1903)
Chest of drawers designed by Moser for his own studio, ca. 1902. (Collection J. Hummel, Vienna)

Perspectival sketches for the interior of a child's bedroom, ca. 1903. (Collection J. Hummel, Vienna)

Wall plan, ca. 1903. (Collection J. Hummel, Vienna)

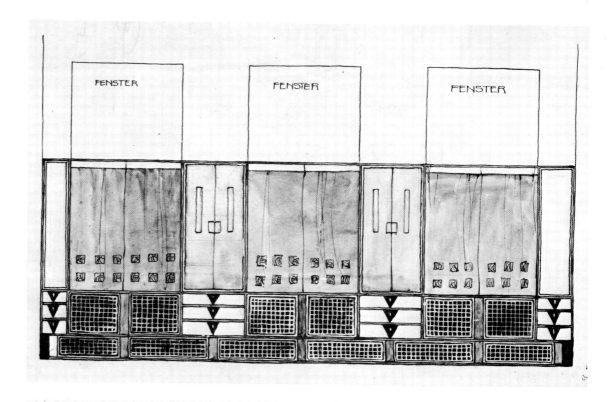

Wall plan, ca. 1903. (Private Collection, Vienna)

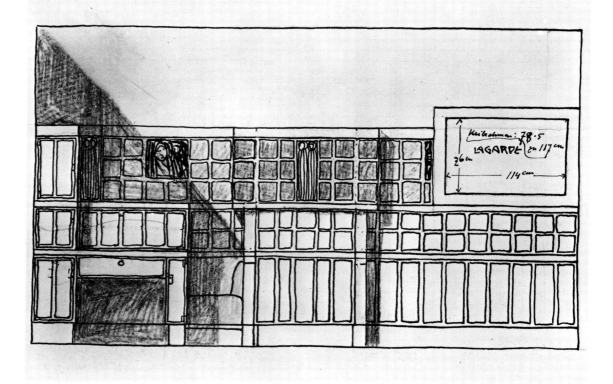

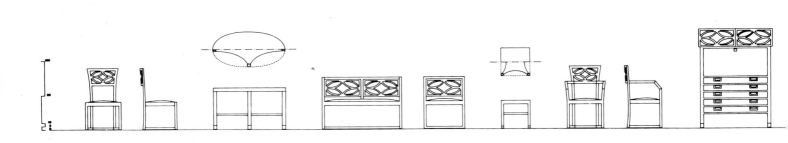

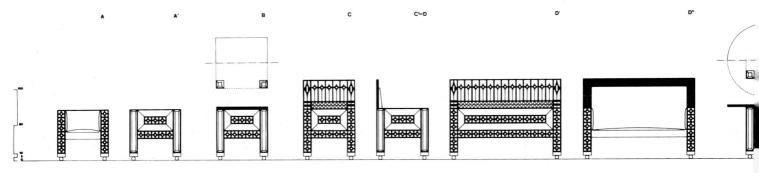

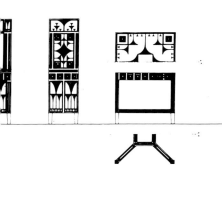

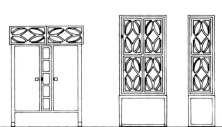

From left: Graphic reconstruction of the furniture planned by Moser for the boudoir and the living room of the "House for a Young Couple," 1903-04, and for the living room of the Koller House, Vienna, 1904. Reconstructive pattern and the "decorational" module provide either a visual order to the interiors and Moser's furniture, as an explicative articulation, or an order for dimensional and functional referents.

In the photographs: The boudoir desk with inlays of two kinds of precious wood, and living room armchair and table in wood inlaid with ebony, mother-of-pearl, coral, etc. (From *Dekorative Kunst*, n. 9, 1904); two chairs and elliptical table for the living room of the Koller House. (From *Archiv der Wiener Werkstätte*, Museum für angewandte Kunst, Vienna)

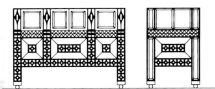

Installation for the Klimt Room at the Vienna Secession's Exhibit XVIII, 1903.

Installation of the Klimt room at the Kunstschau, Vienna, 1908.

Figure study, ca. 1906. (Private Collection, Vienna)

Sketches for stage sets, ca. 1911.
(Private Collection, Vienna)

Abstract frieze, in *Ver Sacrum*, 1901.

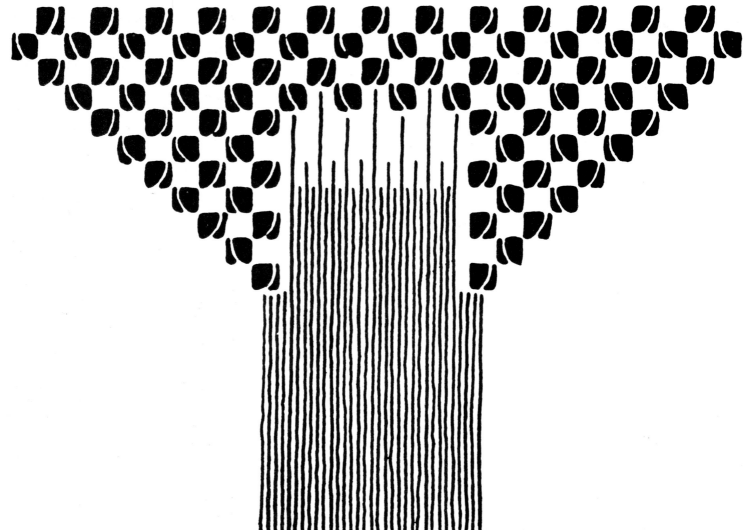

Bibliography

H. Bahr, *Sezession*, Vienna, 1900.

L. Abels, "Koloman Moser," in *Die Kunst*, IV, 1901.

J. Hoffmann, "Einfache Möbel," in *Das Interieur*, II, 1901.

B. Zuckerkandl, "Koloman Moser," in *Dekorative Kunst*, XII, 1903-04.

A.S. Levetus, "An Austrian Decorative Artist: Koloman Moser," in *The Studio*, vol. 33, November 1904.

J.A. Lux, "Josef Hoffmann, Kolo Moser (Wiener Werkstätte)," in *Deutsche Kunst und Dekoration*, XV, 1904-05.

H. Muthesius, *Das englische Haus*, 3 vols, Berlin, 1904 (English translation, *The English House*, London, 1979).

J. Hoffmann, "Das Arbeits Programm der Wiener Werkstätte," in *Hohe Warte*, I, 1904-05.

L. Hevesi, *Acht Jahre Sezession (Marz 1897—Juni 1905) Kritik, Polemik, Chronik*, Vienna, 1905.

The Art Revival in Austria, edited by C. Holme, special issue of *The Studio*, London, 1906.

A.S. Levetus, "Modern Decorative Art in Austria," in *The Art Revival in Austria*.

B. Zuckerkandl, *Zeitkunst—Wien 1901-1907*, Vienna/Leipzig, 1908.

L. Hevesi, *Altkunst-Neukunst: Wien 1894-1908*, Vienna, 1909.

M. Eisler, *Österreichische Werkkultur*, edited by the Österreichische Werkbund, Vienna, 1916.

K. Moser, "Mein Werdegang," in *Velhagen und Klasings Monatshefte*, X, 1916.

H. Bahr, *Tagebuch 1918*, Innsbruck, 1919.

Die Wiener Werkstätte, 1903-1928—Moderne Kunstgewerbe und sein Weg, Vienna, 1929.

S. Tschudi-Madsen, *The Sources of Art Nouveau*, New York, 1956.

R. Schmutzler, *Art Nouveau—Jugendstil*, Stuttgart, 1962.

R. Feuchtmuller and W. Mrazek, *Kunst in Österreich 1860-1918*, Vienna, 1964.

Wien um 1900, Vienna, 1964.

R. Waissenberger, *Wien und die Kunst in unserem Jahrhundert*, Vienna, 1965.

W. Hoffmann, *Moderne Malerei in Österreich*, Vienna, 1965.

Die Wiener Werkstätte—Modernes Kunsthandwerk von 1903-1932, Österreichisches Museum für angewandte Kunst, Vienna, 1967.

W. Hoffmann, "Klimt e la Secessione viennese," in *L'arte moderna*, vol. VII, Milan, 1967.

Kolo Moser, Malerei und Graphik, exhibition catalog, Neue Galerie am Landesmuseum Joanneum, edited by W. Fenz, Graz, 1969.

H.-H. Kossatz, *Ornamentale Plakatkunst—Wiener Judendstil 1897-1914*, Salzburg, 1970.

W. Fenz, "Kolo Moser und die Zeitschrift *Ver Sacrum*," in *Alte und Moderne Kunst*, n. 108, 1970.

H.-H. Kossatz, "The Vienna Secession and Its Early Relations with Great Britain," in *Studio International*, n. 17/6, January 1971.

F. Whitford, "Ends and Beginnings: Viennese Art at the Turn of the Century," in *Studio International*, n. 17/6, January 1971.

Kolo Moser 1868-1918, Ölbilder, Zeichnungen, Kunsthandwerk, catalog, Galerie Nebehay, edited by C.M. Nebehay, Vienna, 1971.

R. Waissenberger, *Die Wiener Sezession*, Vienna, 1971.

J. Hoffmann, "Selbstbiographie," in *Ver Sacrum—Neue Folge* Vienna/Munich, 1972.

E.F Sekler, "Mackintosh and Vienna," in *Architectural Review*, December 1968, now in *The Anti-Rationalist*, edited by N. Pevsner and J.M. Richards, London, 1973.

A. Janik and S. Toulmin, *Wittgenstein's Vienna*, 1973.

P. Vergo, *Art in Vienna*, London, 1975.

C.M. Nebehay, *Ver Sacrum 1898-1903*, Vienna, 1975.

W. Fenz, *Kolo Moser—Internationaler Jugendstil und Wiener Sezession*, Salzburg, 1976.

200 Jahre Mode in Wien—Aus den Modesammlungen des Museums der Stadt, Vienna, 1976.

Ein Dokument Deutscher Kunst—Darmstadt 1901-1976, Darmstadt, 1976-77.

R. Billcliffe and P. Vergo, "Charles Rennie Mackintosh and the Austrian Art Revival," in *The Burlington Magazine*, n. 896, vol CXIX, November 1977.

Vienna Moderne: 1898-1918, exhibition catalog at Sarah Campbell Blaffer Gallery of the University of Houston, Texas, and The Cooper-Hewitt Museum, The Smithsonian Institution's National Museum of Design in New York, 1978-79.

Koloman Moser 1868-1918, exhibition catalog, Hochschule für angewandte Kunst, edited by O. Oberhuber and J. Hummel, with texts by J. Spalt, W. Mrazek, and W.J. Schweiger, Vienna, 1979.

Gebogenes Holz—Konstruktive Entwürfe Wien 1840-1910, Kunstlerhaus, Vienna, 1979.

Vienna—Turn of the Century Art and Design, exhibition catalog, London, 1979-80.

Moderne Vergangenheit 1800-1900, Vienna, 1981.

D. Baroni and A. D'Auria, *Josef Hoffmann e la Wiener Werkstätte*, Milan, 1981.

G. Fanelli and E. Godoli, *La Vienna di Hoffmann, architetto della qualità*, Rome/Bari, 1981.

C. Schorske, *Wien—Geist und Gesellschaft im Fin de Siècle*, Frankfurt am Main, 1979.

W. Johnston, *Vienna Vienna...*, Milan, 1981.

W.J. Schweiger, *Wiener Werkstätte—Kunst und Kunsthandwerk 1903-1932*, Vienna, 1982.

E.F. Sekler, *Josef Hoffmann—Das architektonische Werk*, Salzburg, 1982.

G. Fanelli, "L'infinito ornamento," in *FMR*, n. 8, 1982.

Kolo Moser—Maler und Designer, Galerie Metropol, Vienna/New York, 1982-83.

Ver Sacrum—Die Zeitschrift der Wiener Sezession 1898-1903, Vienna, 1982-83.

Vienna 1900—Vienna, Scotland and the European Avant-garde, Edinburgh, 1983.

"Josef Hoffmann and the Wiener Werkstätte," special issue of *Japan Interior Design*, edited by D. Baroni and A. D'Auria, n. 286, January 1983.

S. Wichmann, *Jugendstil Floral-Funktional*, exhibition catalog, Bayerisches Nationalmuseum, Munich, 1984.

W. Fenz, *Koloman Moser—Graphik Kunstgewerbe Malerei*, Salzburg/Vienna, 1984.

Le arti a Vienna—Dalla Secessione alla caduta dell'impero asburgico, exhibition catalog, Venice Biennale, Milan, 1984.

Group of artists photographed during the installation of the Secession's Exposition XIV dedicated to *Beethoven* by Max Klinger, in 1902. Recognizable from the left are: Anton Stark, Gustav Klimt, Kolo Moser (in front of Klimt with hat), Adolf Böhm, Maximilian Lenz, Ernst Stöhr, Wilhelm List, Emil Orlik (seated), Maxim Kurzweil, Leopold Stolba, Carl Moll and Rudolph Bacher.

The authors wish to give special thanks to Prof. Oswald Oberhuber and to Dr. Erika Patka, rector and director, respectively, of the Archives at the Hochschule für angewandte Kunst in Vienna, for allowing access to priceless and unpublished material; to Dr. Hanna Egger, head librarian for the Österreichisches Museum für angewandte Kunst, for significantly facilitating our research; to Julius Hummel and to the Kunstverlag Wolfrum for putting at our disposal material of great interest; to the Galerie Belle Etage of Vienna; to the architect Amedeo La Nave and to Gennaro Capalbo in the Interior Design course of Prof. Filippo Alison of the School of Architecture, Naples, for editing the graphics; to Dr. Gertrude Kothanek of the Austrian Consulate of Milan for her patient, intelligent support and assistance in all of the research; and to Dr. Elizabetta Pastore of the Italian Consulate of Vienna.

Finally, the authors express their gratitude to Dr. Heinz Adamek, headmaster of the Hochschule für angewandte Kunst, for the valuable aid in research and in contacts with the agencies, institutions and private collectors in Vienna.

Finito di stampare nell'ottobre 1986
presso le Arti Grafiche Leva A&G di Sesto S. Giovanni (MI)
per conto delle Nuove Edizioni Gabriele Mazzotta s.r.l.

DATE DUE	
MAR 1 6 1994	
APR 2 4 1996	
APR 1 4 2004	

GAYLORD   PRINTED IN U.S.A.